GABRIELA MISTRAL

The Teacher from the Valley of Elqui

To Gabriela Mistral
and to the mothers and children
of the world to whom she
dedicated her life.

Gabriela Mistral with the author of this book,
in Roslyn Harbor, New York.

GABRIELA MISTRAL
The Teacher from the Valley of Elqui

by

Marie-Lise Gazarian-Gautier

FRANCISCAN HERALD PRESS

1434 WEST 51st STREET ● CHICAGO, 60609

Gabriela Mistral, the Teacher from the Valley of Elqui was originally published by Editorial Crespillo, Buenos Aires, Argentina, under the title of Gabriela Mistral, la maestra de Elqui by Marie-Lise Gazarian-Gautier. The English translation from the Spanish was done by the author. Copyright © 1975, Franciscan Herald Press, 1434 West 51st St., Chicago, Illinois 60609.

Library of Congress Cataloging in Publication Data:

Gazarian-Gautier, Marie-Lise.
   Gabriela Mistral, the Teacher from the Valley of Elqui.
   Translation of Gabriela Mistral, la maestra de Elqui.
   Bibliography: p.
   Includes index.
   1. Godoy Alcayaga, Lucila, 1889-1957—Biography.
I. Title.
PQ8097.G6Z56413   861 B   75-4764
ISBN 0-8199-0544-5

MADE IN THE UNITED STATES OF AMERICA

To Gabriela Mistral
and the mothers and children
of the world to whom she dedicated
her life, and in memory of
Palma Guillen de Nicolau,
her long-time Mexican friend.

Acknowledgements

I would like to express my gratitude to my family and my friends for their constant encouragement and extend a special word of thanks to my Chilean friend Francisca Santa Cruz de Thais for her sincere interest in this biography of her great compatriot Gabriela Mistral.

M-L G.G.
Orient, Long Island

Contents

Preface

Song to St. Francis

*"Francis, I would like to pass among
things without disturbing a single petal.
Let there remain within them but a slight
murmur and the gentle remembrance they
have of me."*

GABRIELA MISTRAL

ᴗᴑᴖᴗᴑᴖᴗᴑᴖᴗᴑᴖᴗᴑᴖᴗᴑᴖᴗᴑᴖᴗᴑᴖᴗᴑᴖᴗᴑᴖᴗᴑᴖᴗᴑᴖᴗᴑᴖᴗᴑᴖᴗᴑᴖᴗᴑᴖᴗᴑᴖ

Lucila Godoy y Alcayaga, who wrote as Gabriela Mistral (1889-1957), won the Nobel Prize for Literature in 1945 for her poetry in general, but specifically for the volume entitled *Desolación*. A Chilean, she shared the Catholic faith of the majority of her countrymen, but she also realized that, as her biographer Dr. Marie-Lise Gazarian-Gautier puts it so succinctly, "a fundamental element of Christianity was missing in the daily practice of religion: social awareness and social justice." This Gabriela Mistral realized as early as 1924 when she wrote that Christianity was "meant for the people. . . . If we are total Christians of the total Gospel, we will go to the people," for though "poverty is no enemy to spiritual progress, misery is."

The Chilean writer saw in every oppressed man, woman, or child the face of God. She compared the poor homeless children of her American continent to the Child Jesus who had been denied a lodging and she tried to awake in well-to-do people a sense of sharing: "The child who sleeps in the frost and in the stormy snow drift is not just an engraving made of plaster or a Christmas card." She saw in Mary the familiar face of her own mother.

Gabriela Mistral was a Franciscan Tertiary and St. Francis of Assisi was her favorite saint. Like him, she knew humility, placed Christ at the center of her life, and joyfully loved all created things. She was a sister to trees and herbs and partook of the

xi

inner secrets of the earth. She once wrote in a letter: "I am a Christian, an advocate of democracy. . . . I come from peasant stock and am a peasant."

Like St. Francis, she strove throughout her life to strip herself of all she possessed in order to give back to others what had been given her. She said in a poem written in her latter period:

If they place close by me
a born blind girl,
I will tell her, softly, so softly,
with a voice filled with dust:
—Sister, take my eyes.

Let another take my arms
if she be maimed.
And others take my senses
with their thirst and their hunger.

Let me thus be consumed,
shared like a loaf of bread,
hurled from north to south
I shall never again be one.

Indeed, Gabriela Mistral is remembered in all of Latin America not only as a great poet, but as an apostle to the poor and the oppressed. She grew up in a tiny village, Monte Grande, of almost biblical simplicity. She taught first in rural schools, later in high schools. In 1922 she went to Mexico to participate in the reform movement in Mexican education, whose initiator was José Vasconcelos. In 1932, she joined the Chilean consular service and worked in various countries, finally coming to New York, where she spent the last years of her life. Her remains are interred in Monte Grande, in her native Chile.

Marie-Lise Gazarian-Gautier has studied Gabriela Mistral's prose as well as her poetry. She knew the poet personally during the last years of Gabriela's life and would sit by her side, a young girl dressed in blue, devoted to the great woman, dedicated to the great writer. It was then that Gabriela Mistral called her "La Niña Azul," "a girl of the color of the sky."

This account of Gabriela's life, work and thought is profound and perceptive, and we are fortunate indeed to become acquainted with the Chilean mystic and humanitarian through the words of so sensitive, so devout, and so articulate a biographer.

ANNE FREMANTLE
Mexico City, April 1974

Introduction

"My small literary work is Chilean in its sense of measure and in its vigor. It has never been the sole aim of my life. What I have done is to teach and to live among my young girls. . . . I come from peasant stock and am a peasant. My great loves are my faith, the earth, and poetry."

GABRIELA MISTRAL

Gabriela Mistral is the first Latin American poet to have received the Nobel Prize. However she is remembered in her native Chile and throughout Latin America not only because she was a great poet and prose writer who made her continent famous, but also because she was an apostle of the poor and the oppressed. Throughout her life her home was always open to all, and often became a refuge for the afflicted. Visitors from many countries came to see her and found true friendship tendered by an outstretched hand. She treated everyone with the utmost frankness, one of her most characteristic traits, which she perhaps inherited from her Basque ancestry. She never hesitated to call things by their rightful names. Though she attached little importance to the material aspects of life, her writings were rooted in reality, in the land and the people she knew so well. She was a realist even though she was surrounded by mystery and poetry. Her life and work cannot be separated. They are filled with the same poetry and the same passion for justice. Gabriela Mistral, the woman, the educator, the fighter for social justice, and the writer, are all one.

Her childhood was spent in the small village of Monte Grande in the Valley of Elqui, where she lived with her mother and her half sister. It was her home that nourished her poetic language, both in poetry and prose, her deep passion for the earth, and her mystic flights toward God.

As an educator, she rose from the position of teacher in rural schools to that of teacher and later director in secondary schools. Essentially self-taught, her bitter and sometimes happy experiences helped her to guide and care for the young and the oppressed. Much of her poetry and her prose has an educational purpose: to impart a sense of beauty, as well as to bring about reforms.

The cultural and diplomatic phase of her work began in 1922 when she left Chile to take part in the movement for educational reforms in Mexico. Four years later, she went to Europe to participate in the work of the International Institute of Intellectual Cooperation in Paris and of the League of Nations in Geneva.

During her consular career, which began in 1932, she served consecutively as consul in Spain, Portugal, France, Brazil, Santa Barbara (California), Mexico, Italy and New York. Because her activities as an educator and diplomat called her to various countries, she never again lived permanently in her native land.

In 1945, Gabriela Mistral was awarded the Nobel Prize for Literature. Following this highest recognition, various other honors were bestowed upon her, including the Chilean National Prize for Literature and the Degree of Doctorate *Honoris Causa* from several American and European universities.

She spent the last years of her life in Roslyn Harbor, New York, recalling in the beautiful pages of her *Poema de Chile* (Poem about Chile) the fruits, the flowers, the woodlands, the mountains, and the sea of her beloved country. She died on January 10, 1957, and her remains were moved first to Santiago and finally in 1960 to Monte Grande, the small village of her childhood.

Gabriela Mistral often said that her two functions in life were to write and to teach. Throughout her life these went hand in hand. Actually, she preferred to think of herself as a rural schoolteacher rather than as a writer. Her dreams, as she expressed it in 1925, would have been to have a small school in the Valley of Elqui where she could have raised goats and led a simple but rich inner life. At the time of her death she was revered in Chile both as a poet and as a teacher.

Her first impulse to write seems to have been her desire to further the total development of her pupils, her children as she called them. It was her concern for children, the sight of their inadequate textbooks, that made her write poetry and prose for them. She sought to awaken in children and teachers a spiritual and intellectual rebirth through their discovery of the beauty of nature around them and of the famous American men and women of the past and present whose lives have been filled with the spirit of God. She wanted young people to become aware of their surroundings, to know in depth the features of their own country as well as those of all other Latin American nations because they were part of the same people. Gabriela advocated freedom in teaching without any rigid curriculum, for she remembered that as a teacher she had often been restricted by set rules that imprisoned her creative power.

Gabriela Mistral had a religious attitude toward every aspect of life. She was a teacher in the deepest meaning of the word. She embraced in her love of children the unborn child and all expectant mothers. She cared for the child's body and soul, his complete development, seen in the context of his spiritual union with his family, his home, and his teachers. She favored a Christian and democratic school where, as in the Gospels, the love of the poor and the feeling of charity are expressed. Such a school, she felt, reveals the need for unity among social classes. It was fundamentally important to her that rich and poor children study side by side. The school was to her a sacred place, just as the church or temple, and the home. She felt that each school was a spiritual creation that guides children who are the world's only salvation.

Gabriela was also deeply interested in adult education and especially concerned with the development of rural people in the small villages of Latin America. She wanted to see the life of the peasant ennobled through specialized schools and through libraries, art exhibits, and recreation. These would bring about a spiritual awakening and contribute toward true democracy. Gabriela believed that through evening classes and a common interest in books all social classes could be drawn together. In the same way, a love of art should be taught, so that beauty and its appreciation would lead men to God. Religion and a deep sense of social justice made her feel a continuous anxiety for the fate of the underprivileged:

"Because I am not an artist; I am a woman in whom there lives the longing to instill in my people, the concept of religion with an overwhelming yearning for social justice which pervades my being. I do not feel for my small literary work to which you have alluded the same burning interest that I feel for the fate of my people."[1]

Time and again, Gabriela would say that she was neither a politician—she always made a point of saying that she had never voted in her life—nor a fighter, even though she defended the rights of women and children. She believed in liberalism and compared it to an avenue of evergreen trees that give shade equally to men of all races. It is interesting to note that in 1930 Gabriela wrote that while she was in Monterrey, Mexico, conservatives considered her a radical and that in the same country, in Michoacan, radicals looked upon her as a bigoted churchgoer. Actually, she was a Christian and a democrat who had a social, moral, and religious concept of life. She believed in the role of women in society, in their rights to intervene for the defense of children and the preservation of peace.

It was in her homeland that Gabriela Mistral first came in contact with nature, with God, and with the social and cultural ideas that encompassed many of the beliefs that became part of her conception of life and death. Yet, it is fair to say that some of her ideals were strengthened as she came to know at first hand the entire American hemisphere and Europe. It was then that she conceived the idea of Latin America as one large country, that she came to understand and advocate love for her Indian brothers and that she defended them through her poetry and her prose. When she received the Nobel Prize, she felt that this great honor was not given to her, but to all the women of Latin America.

Gabriela Mistral is best known as a poet. Yet she must be equally recognized as a prose writer whose work was enriched by the sensitive qualities of the poet. Her prose is often poetic and her poetry has the vitality and strength of the spoken word. She established an intimate bond between poetry and prose.

Whether poetry or prose, her writing bears a strong personal stamp. The themes and the style are unmistakably hers. They are the expression of a deeply religious person who looks back to the Middle Ages to find a true artistic and moral sense and who looks toward the future to bring to our contemporary period a renewed and revitalized faith.

Gabriela Mistral's writing is focused on youth. Beyond the writer there is always the concern of the rural schoolteacher. She had a missionary-like concept of teaching which made her feel that teachers and mothers have similar roles. Although without children of her own, she came to be the mother of all children. Through her teaching and writing she exalted motherhood to a sanctified state. José Vasconcelos, then Minister of Education of Mexico, wrote of her unique quality in understanding people: ". . . Because there is no other woman in our own time more beloved and admired than you, Gabriela, you are the burning light that discovers the secrets of the human soul and the destiny of people."[2]

Both as a poet and a prose writer Gabriela Mistral transmitted a religious message, which was derived from her deep-rooted sense of social justice found in basic Christianity. Her personal love and sorrow evolved into a universal love and an all-embracing understanding of human suffering. Her concern for humanity thus became the motivating force of her writing.

Gabriela's poetry reveals her deep capacity for love, her preoccupation with death, her hope in eternity and in reunion with those she had loved, and her search for God and ultimate oneness with Him. Her act of faith was not handed down to her through dogma, but was a direct face-to-face encounter with God. Her poetry is an expression of her soul, sometimes a direct dialogue between God and herself, sometimes between His creation and herself. Since she knew suffering, poetry became for her a comforting and indispensable companion. It was real and intense, born of her very flesh. What Gabriela said about the veracity of José Martí's poetry could apply to her own and shows to what extent sincerity in art was important to her: "To confess my faith in this supernatural man means simply that I swear blindly to the authenticity of his poetry. His poetry holds among its chain of virtues of a special touch which is seldom found among poets: the touch of the genuine, of a truth that can see and touch even when its object is ineffable and intangible."[3] Her poetry is derived from her life. It is, however, difficult to know where facts leave off and fantasy begins, for poetry transforms and modifies events through the interplay of reality and imagination. Her poetic art is, therefore, sometimes an enigma. Her message goes beyond the actual words.

Gabriela's prose, on the other hand, is less introspective. Her journalistic prose is informative; its aim is to call for action to bring about reforms. Her poetic prose reflects her philosophy of life and is written to awaken young people to a spiritual consciousness and to make them aware of the beauty of the American hemisphere.

Her poetry and her prose are two parallel expressions born of the same spirit. They are an aesthetic and moral affirmation of inner and outer beauty. The themes are often identical, and they are closely related to the basic motivations in her own life. Her vision of the world, like that of St. Francis, encompasses every element of God's creation. She humanizes objects and at times sanctifies them. She finds God in everything.

Gabriela constantly revised her writing in her quest for a pure form of art. Writing was for her a religious experience which drew her closer to God:

"What Christ said of Paradise can also be applied to art: 'Verily I say unto you, whosoever does not become like a child shall not enter the Kingdom of Heaven.' Only after pruning the branches of rhetoric which is the vanity of our songs, only after stripping ourselves of the false glimmer of the expensive jewelry of our language, shall we enter the clear path of true Beauty, and Eternity shall be granted to us as a reward for what we cast aside, for the humility we have embraced."[4]

In both poetry and prose there are similarities in the modes of expression: (1) the use of the *recado* (message) in both literary forms; (2) themes derived from experiences in her life which left a deep mark upon her; (3) a combativeness, directness, even abruptness in approach that reveal her sincerity and her relentless search for truth; (4) the use of a vital vocabulary through which she enriched the Spanish language, bringing to it a new sensitivity, warmth, and intensity, with special stress on the spoken message; (5) religious fervor which was an integral part of her life—the foundation stone and the culmination of all her work.

Gabriela Mistral lives on in her poetry, her prose, and the ideals which she instilled in all those who came within her reach.

Born in Chile she now belongs to the world, and to Latin Americans her voice is one of the most representative of their continent. Jorge Mañach expresses with great insight the literary and spiritual message of Gabriela Mistral:

"In her language of natural baroque—which is a good quality—Gabriela Mistral stands as a spiritual and literary guide. She is one of the living classics of America. But she is more than that: because of the coming together of soul and earth that permeate her work and her life; because of her gift of memory and hope; because of her sensitivity toward the most profound and universal concerns of these new countries; even because of her physical appearance of a heroic stature and gentle weariness, she is like a living incarnation of the Spanish American soul. The whole American land has become spirit through her."[5]

CHAPTER 1

Childhood
and
Youth
in Chile

"Lord, you who taught,
forgive me that I teach,
that I bear the name of teacher,
which you bore on earth."

GABRIELA MISTRAL

GABRIELA MISTRAL, whose real name was Lucila Godoy Alcayaga, was born on April 7, 1889, in the Province of Coquimbo, Chile. This vast northern province is a land of contrasts, fertile and desolate, extending from the Andean heights and valleys to sea level at the Pacific Ocean. It is known for its mines and its agricultural wealth, and as the birthplace of noted Chilean poets, among them Magallanes Moure, Carlos Mondaca, Víctor Domingo Silva, and Julio Muñízaga Ossandón.

Her parents, fearing some difficulties in the child's birth, had left the village of La Unión in the interior (now known as Pisco-Elqui) and come to Vicuña, the capital of the Valley of Elqui. On the day following their arrival, the future poet was born at four o'clock in the morning in a humble house at Calle Maipú 759. The infant was baptized on the day of her birth in the church of the Immaculate Conception of Vicuña and given the name Lucila. The unusual circumstance of birth and baptism on the same day has led to occasional confusion as to the exact date of Gabriela Mistral's birth.

The father, Jerónimo Godoy Villanueva, was a rural schoolteacher who had an extraordinary ability for improvising poetry in the tradition of the classical South American *payadores* or the Spanish troubadours. He had come originally from Atacama, the most rebellious province of northern Chile, a land of legends, of miners, and revolutionary people. In his youth he had studied at

3

the seminary of La Serena, since his mother, Isabel de Villanueva, an austere and religious woman, had hoped he would become a priest. (His two sisters had entered religious orders.) This hope was not realized, but as a result of his seminary training in La Serena, Jerónimo Godoy was a good Latinist and spoke French fluently. He had a happy disposition and was gifted in the arts— in writing poetry, playing the violin and the guitar, and drawing with great facility. Perhaps it was from her father that the future Gabriela Mistral inherited her love of fantasy, her *wanderlust,* and her great passion for folklore.

While Jerónimo Godoy was teaching in Public School No. 10 in the village of La Unión, he met and fell in love with Petronila Alcayaga de Molina, a widow with a daughter, Emelina, then fifteen years old. The couple was married in 1888 in the Parish of Paihuano.

Petronila Alcayaga was a small woman of great beauty. She was to play an important role in the life of the future poet by giving her a warm and loving home life and instilling in her a love of nature. From her closeness with her mother, Gabriela learned as a child to enjoy this intimate relationship with nature, as if every element were a member of her family. Later she would remember each aspect of the valley and would re-create them with onomatopoeic words; the murmurs, the squeaks, the blows of the axe, the perfume of the trees and flowers. Her earthiness dates back to the moment her mother led her by the hand and named each fruit, plant, or tree, or the simple and familiar elements such as water, bread, and salt. The daughter inherited many of the qualities of her mother's Basque ancestors, particularly tenacity of purpose and integrity. She regarded her mother as someone sacred, perhaps because of her mother's suffering in giving her birth; and this religious feeling came to embrace all mothers. Concerning her mother, she wrote: "She was a very beautiful and delicate woman whose moving voice always speaks to my memory as the most perfect human voice I have ever heard. The marvelous charity of her heart arose and spoke through that soft and gentle voice."[1]

The first three years of Lucila's life were happy ones. Her parents loved her. Her father even wrote poems to lull her to sleep and, like her mother, taught her to love nature. He culti-vated a small garden especially for her and perhaps thus initiated her into the search for beauty. Although his poems were never published during his lifetime, they reveal a great soul. Here are three of his cradlesongs dedicated to Lucila:

When you raise your blue eyes
to heaven
tell me, who beckons you
to turn thither?
Whom are you smiling at,
innocent one,
when you joyfully lift
up your eyes?[2]

Oh sweet Lucila,
the clement heavens
witnessed your birth
in bitter days,
perhaps, dear child,
they hold for you
the joy they would not
grant your parents![3]

Sleep Lucila for the world is at peace;
The lamb doesn't frisk, nor does the sheep bleat.
Sleep Lucila for in Heaven God protects you
and in your cradle an Angel cares for you.
Sleep Lucila, my sweetheart,
for your mother is also sleepy.

Guardian Angel, lull her to sleep
let her mother rest untroubled.
Guardian Angel, take care of this lily
for tomorrow at dawn she will pray with me.
Sleep my child, sleep I pray you,
if you do not sleep my anger will be roused.[4]

Since she had been privileged to hear such songs as a child, she later felt compelled to write tender cradlesongs for other children:

"At night I often walk along the streets of my poor district and, coming from the end of a dark corridor, I hear the grotesque verse which, in a very soft melody, the woman from the common people sings—the most loving of mothers—lulling her child to sleep.

"And my soul is bathed in tenderness when I remember that I, a happier child than this one, had other songs: four or five songs that my father wrote for his wife to rock me to sleep. Perhaps they are not beautiful; they are soft and plain, nothing more. Why more?

"Then I think it is my duty to give back to mothers their songs, four other songs in exchange for those that fell softly and gently upon my crib like the moon's bright rays."[5]

Jerónimo Godoy, despite this brief period of happiness, felt again and again the urge to wander and the call of adventure. He would leave his home from time to time and come back as though nothing had happened. Her parents' unhappy marriage left a deep impression on little Lucila; nevertheless, she always remembered her father with great admiration: "My recollection of him could be tinted with bitterness because of his absence, but it is filled with admiration for the many things he was and with a profound filial love."[6]

In later years, she, too, was to feel the same need for wandering and she became a constant traveler. In fact, in her conversations with friends, she would make fun of herself, and she invented the word *"patiloca"* (itchy feet) to express this need for movement. She enjoyed giving nicknames to herself as well as to her friends.

Lucila was only three years old when her father finally deserted his family and it was then that her half sister Emelina Molina de Barraza took the place in her life that he had occupied. Like her stepfather, Emelina was a rural schoolteacher. She had entered the profession in 1889 and was to continue teaching for more than thirty years. By the time of her retirement in 1926 she had taught in Elqui, Monte Grande, Diaguitas, Paihuano, El Molle, Los Andes, and La Serena. In 1892 she was appointed teacher in the rural school of Monte Grande, a small village in the center of the Valley of Elqui, high in the Andes Mountains, and her mother and sister came to live with her there. This narrow valley, hemmed in by mountains and born out of the very metal of the Cordillera, was inhabited by persevering and sturdy people who through their labor changed the soil into a generous verdant pasture, rich in luxuriant fruits: ". . . What a beautiful life full of emotions amidst our untamed mountains. Eyes thirsty for light and shapes, ears that draw in the winds and waters was what we harvested from those villages that work the soil. They hold on to it with love and find solace in the countryside with a spiritual and corporeal bliss unknown to the learned cities hardened by every day turmoil."[7]

Emelina was by this time a widow, and when she lost her own daughter Graciela—in whose memory Gabriela was to write a beautiful poem—she transferred all ·her love to her young half sister. Within a month's time she had gone through a whole speller with Lucila, had taught her to read, and had given her some beginning lessons in writing ànd arithmetic. As the years went by, Emelina was to be the main source of Lucila's formal education: "Holy Sister Emelina who was my only true teacher, apostolic soul, who inspired my poem 'The Rural School-teacher.' "[8]

Lucila was a handsome child, with blue eyes, flecked with green, who lived within herself, and whose playmates were the domestic animals, the insects, the birds, and the plants. How often her mother would call her and find her talking with an iguana, or with a tree, or shaping little figurines in clay, or standing still in wrapt contemplation of nature.[9] Her mother said of her: "How many times Lucila left my arms to run to the garden and there remain in mute contemplation among the almond trees in bloom! How many times I caught her in an intimate conversation with birds and flowers!"[10]

Monte Grande became for the little girl her true home, the landscape of her childhood, where she learned to play, to meditate, and to come into close contact with God and all that He had created: ". . . The truth is that I consider my homeland the village prior to La Unión, where I spent my childhood from the age of three to nine and which is called Monte Grande, the village where my sister Emelina was a rural schoolteacher at that time. I believe that the land of childhood is the true homeland. (I use the word homeland meaning region)."[11]

The patriarchal customs of Monte Grande, isolated in the lofty Valley of Elqui, made life easier for the two women and the child. Representing almost three generations, they maintained a deep family relationship through love and hard work. They lived humbly, but there was no painful separation of classes in the little village. The mother helped those with greater wealth to distribute it better among the needy. She would often send her little girl Lucila to some well-to-do neighbor to ask him to give some of his many apples or other fruit to those who did not have any. In that way, everyone could enjoy the bountiful fruits of this semitropical land—its peaches, apricots, pears, oranges, grapes, papayas, damsons, pomegranates, figs, walnuts, and olives. "The earth provided men with everything they asked from it: light, water, wine, and fruits. And what fruits! The tongue that has tasted the nectar from its peaches and the mouth that has bitten into its mulberry colored fig will not want to try another for none can be sweeter."[12]

In this land and among its lively people the future poet spent her formative years and received from them a feeling of closeness with the Creator. One critic has justly said that in the Valley of Elqui one immediately becomes conscious of the grandeur of nature and that because of it one can feel, touch, and see God.[13] As one enters the valley one feels that everything, including man or plant, tends to stretch toward the sky and toward the light, in an outburst of spiritual exaltation. All is serene and pure: the earth, the rocks, the hills, the water, the sky, and the stars are so bright that they light up the way at night. Perhaps because of all these elements the people are joyful, friendly, and generous. In later years Gabriela Mistral often recounted to me how her mother would stand at the door of her house and joyfully invite any passerby to share a maté tea with her. She was witty and liked company. The Chilean writer Benjamín Subercaseaux thus describes that region:

"This region reminds us of the biblical land: goats like those found in the East look down from every rock and at every turn of the road. . . . Vineyards resemble those of Jericho; the fig tree of the gospels shows everywhere its tormented outline, and the donkey walks along the dusty roads with the same dull and dreary meekness as the one from the Holy Family. Has it not been said that Gabriela Mistral herself has an inflection that recalls that of the prophets of old?"[14]

In her thirst for nature the young Lucila found an inexhaustible source of knowledge in Adolfo Iribarren, a wealthy landholder of Monte Grande. Iribarren, of Basque origin, had a deep interest in the plant and animal kingdoms and had transformed his property into a veritable botanical garden and zoological park. He would let Lucila play among the exotic plants and make companions of the deer, gazelles, peacocks, and pheasants. Thus he introduced her to a world until then unknown to her and, in part, foreign to the Valley of Elqui: ". . . There I came to know many exotic trees, among them the Puerto Rican 'flamboyant' which he called by its real name of 'fire tree' and which truly blazed when it blossomed not less than the bonfire."[15]

He would tell her stories about each species, explain the various parts of the world, and even initiated her into astronomy. In this way he enlivened the already bright imagination of the child. Lucila by then had reached the age of nine and received her first Communion. She is said to have shown her first writings to others at that time. Later in her life, Gabriela Mistral revealed to me her deep interest in science and often said that if she could have chosen her vocation again she would rather have been a scientist than a poet. Whether or not this could have been possible is not important; she was certainly akin to Sister Juana Inés de la Cruz, the seventeenth century Mexican poet, in her constant quest for knowledge, no matter what the field.

Because of these happy years, Monte Grande, as well as the whole Valley of Elqui, became for the future poet an earthly paradise which she carried in her heart wherever she went, and whose images form the subsoil of all her poetry. She loved her village as one loves a friend and she knew it so well that she possessed it and preserved it completely in her memory. She once said that she needed to extend love even to a village.[16] During all her life Gabriela Mistral would try to find a similar climate and similar people in whatever country her work took her. This feeling of love and nostalgia for her people and her *patria chiquita* (tiny home region) was to grow stronger with the years. I remember with what warmth she spoke to me of the fruits, the flowers, the mild weather of the beloved region of her youth. In spite of her long absence, partly because the high altitude was dangerous for her health, it remained as vivid to her as if she had lived there all her life. In deepening our insight into the atmosphere of the Valley of Elqui, we can better understand the poetic language and spirit of Gabriela Mistral, her deep passion for the earth, and her mystic flight toward God.

The Valley of Elqui has mountains
that search for God upon awakening
that seek God at night
and find Him at dawn,
and praise Him at daybreak.
They are high and beautiful,
they praise Him the whole day
and keep vigil with Him as night falls.
When I was small they awoke me
with their soft and fervent sun,
their psalms of light still
recall the eternal prayer.[17]

This happy and peaceful life ended when Lucila was sent to Vicuña to finish her last year of primary school. Until then, she had felt at home in the small school of Monte Grande where, as she studied under her half sister's guidance and love, she was never made conscious of her extreme shyness. The school at Vicuña was directed by a friend of her mother, Adelaida Olivares, who, being a blind woman, took the child as a little companion. She made Lucila walk with her from school to her house and back, and also assigned to her the task of distributing paper for lessons to her classmates. Perhaps because Adelaida Olivares was blind, she never understood how timid and sensitive Lucila was and to what extent she lived in an inner world. The children took advantage of Lucila and used up the supply of paper too fast, making her appear responsible. Gabriela Mistral would often talk of this bitter episode of her life—how because of her shyness her name "Lucila Godoy" would sound when she spoke something like "Totilla Llolloy" and she could not defend herself from the accusations and the stones of the other children. This first and profound encounter with human cruelty and injustice left a lasting mark on the future teacher and poet, for she understood that she would have to fight for the rights of the defenseless, the humble, and the poor. Lucila was sent home and once more found in her half sister Emelina a true, unselfish guide whose love she was to repay in her beautiful portrayal of her in the poem "La maestra rural" (The Rural Schoolteacher): "I owe everything that I know and that I am to my devoted and unselfish sister Emelina, who educated me at home, taking time from her hours of rest".[18]

Lucila spent the first twelve years of her life in the country, but around 1901 her family moved to La Serena, the capital of the Province of Coquimbo, an ancient city, rich in traditions, on the Pacific Coast at the entrance to the Valley of Elqui. It was there that she had her first encounter with the sea, an element that is felt in all her poetry and that together with the mountains is reflected in both the Chilean people and the geography of the country:

"A territory so small that on the map it seems to be a beach between the chain of mountains and the sea, a parenthesis or play with space, between the two dominating centaurs. . . .

"A small territory, not a small nation: an abridged land, inferior to the ambition and the heroic nature of its people. It does not matter: we have the sea. . . . the seas. . . . the sea. . . . !"[19]

"The sea has given us all the possibilities in almost four thousand five hundred kilometers of sea coast. It is at any point within one's reach, six hours from the city or from the village encased in the mountains; we possess such a proximity with the sea that, even though we come from the rough mountains, it can be said that the sea air has strengthened the lungs of all our people and has given us a deeper and more enduring spirit."[20]

The sea was not for Lucila an impersonal element, but a powerful being with whom she conversed and whom she called "father." By studying the formation of each wave, its color and its rhythm, she would embrace in the same love everything that was related to, or part of it: the salt, the algae, the marine snail, the small boats, and the fishermen. If she understood the sea, the sea in turn understood her and would rock her to sleep, giving her consolation and joy in its music and in its mysterious expression of the Eternal.

> *Take me, adopt me, give me*
> *your salt, your dance, your rhythm,*
> *and dispel from me all harbors.*
> *My father the sea receives me*
> *with his all-embracing foam.*
> *May he give me the wisdom*
> *of his law and his echo*
> *and may his music follow me*
> *and give shape to my second body.* [21]

In La Serena, Lucila's paternal grandmother, Isabel de Villa-nueva, was to play a fundamental part in her development by kindling in her heart a fiery and passionate thirst for God and the life beyond. Isabel was a religious woman, whose family came from Argentina and who, because she was the only woman in La Serena who owned a Bible, was said to be of Jewish extraction. Gabriela Mistral, who possessed the strength of the Basque people and the gentleness and melancholy of the Indians, liked to believe that she also had in her makeup the tenacity of the Jews. Often she would recall for me the way her mother would dress her up on Sundays and send her to her grandmother, whose sight was poor. She would sit by her side and read her passages of the Bible. Thus, she became acquainted with the Book of Job, the Psalms, Ecclesiastes, the Lamentations of Jeremiah, the Song of Songs, the Book of Revelation; they became so familiar to her that they left a deep mark on her soul and on her writings. Job, David, Solomon, and the other prophets revealed themselves as friends who had suffered and fought and who had known a deep and violent passion for God. King David was her first and great love. She found in the Old and the New Testaments not only spiritual nourishment but also human beings and landscapes close to her own self and to her own people. She was reminded of scenes of her childhood, where she learned to love and appreciate the simple things of life, to withstand suffering with forbearance, and to be merciful, gentle, and even violent at times: "My best friends have not been people of my time, but those that you gave me: David, Ruth, Job, Rachel, and Mary. Together with my people they are my sole companions, those who watch over my heart and my prayers, those who help me to love and accept suffering." [22]

From this time on and in spite of financial difficulties, Lucila read with frenzy all the books she could find; she borrowed them from a friendly Spanish storeowner, and was offered the use of the library of a wealthy and generous neighbor. She learned everything through an immediate and personal contact with people and things, and it was through this constant studying rather than formal schooling that she became selfeducated. Perhaps it was because she could only read the books that came into her hands and thus could not be as selective as had she studied under literary guidance, that she was so taken by the then very popular Colombian writer José María Vargas Vila (1860-1933) whom in 1905 she considered her master. Fortunately, this blind attraction for his morbid and artificial style was counterbalanced by the sincerity and vital realism she had found in the Scriptures: the fiery metaphors, the apostrophes of the prophets, the truly-felt cries of passion.

When she was eleven years old, she wrote a poem to her friend Dolores Molina whom she called Lola. However, it was probably in 1904, when she was fourteen, that she became conscious of her desire to write and some of her prose material began to be published in *El Coquimbo* of La Serena and in *La Voz de Elqui,* edited in Vicuña. These pieces were impregnated with romantic elements; they appeared somewhat revolutionary to the provincial set and may have been the reason for her failure to gain admission to the Normal School (Teachers' College) of La Serena. Lucila had been admitted and then refused, without explanation, by its chaplain, Manuel Ignacio Munizaga.[23] This was another blow and a bitter experience, for it meant that she could not pursue specialized studies to become a teacher. The teacher's career was the only one within her reach, and she had inherited from her father and her half sister a gift for it. In spite of this unjust obstacle placed in her path, she undertook on her own the painful apprenticeship of the teaching profession through practical experience.

In 1905, at the age of fifteen, she began to work. Her first position was as a clerk in the Public High School of La Serena, which was attended mainly by the children of the upper bourgeoisie. Her deep Christian spirit rebelled against the separation of classes, and because she accepted some young girls from modest homes and defended their equal rights she was forced to leave. "Alas! I know well what it means to be thrown out."[24] In her despair she was said to have sought the advice of her great friend, the sea. On her way there, she met the governor of the province, who noticed the sad adolescent and spoke to her. Learning of her distress, he appointed her as an assistant in the rural school of La Compañía Baja, about three kilometers from La Serena.[25] This was her first teaching post. She taught the poor children during the day and the workers at night, and was thanked by them on Sunday with their folk songs. Although she was little more than a child, she fully realized the importance and the beauty of her mission. In this personal contact with the young and with the humble of the working class, she was spiritually enriched as she united this feeling of love for God's creatures with her already deep identification with nature. She was to remain a primary schoolteacher from 1905 to 1910. During all her life, Gabriela Mistral felt herself above all a simple rural teacher who had written songs for her numerous pupils, with the Valley of Elqui as a background, and she was happier to be remembered as a teacher than to be thought of as a poet or as a diplomat. She taught for more than twenty years and until the end of her life she was a spiritual guide to all who came within her reach: "I was brought up in the country until the age of twelve. The rural life has persisted in me and I continue to take an interest in country schools and even in agrarian matters. I began teaching as a rural schoolteacher at the age of fifteen. . . ."[26]

Beginning in 1905 Lucila's writings, both prose and poetry, appeared frequently in the provincial press and were often signed with the pseudonyms of "Alguien" (Someone), "Soledad" (Solitude), and "Alma" (Soul). They reflected the sad, melancholy spirit of South American writers of the 1900's.[27] An example is a poem written by her in the album of her friend Lola (Dolores Molina):

> *Tell me why you call on my songs?*
> *Don't you see that my soul inhabits darkness?*
> *Don't you see that you ask from unplowed land a*
>   *flower?*
> *Don't you see that you ask from the night the dawn?*[28]

In 1907 Lucila was transferred to the school of La Cantera, a hamlet consisting of some thirty white houses between the port of Coquimbo and La Serena. She was then a tall, fairhaired girl of seventeen. Her eyes were blue-green and her hands were so graceful that they were compared to a lily.[29] It was probably while in La Cantera that she met Romelio Ureta, an employee in the local railroad, whose suicide on November 25, 1909 was to inspire some vibrant pages in the section "Dolor" (Sorrow) of *Desolación* (Desolation), her first book. Romelio Ureta died in Coquimbo while Lucila was in Santiago. He killed himself in despair at not being able to replace a sum of money he had taken from his company for his friend Carlos Omar Barrios.[30] Because

an old card with Lucila's signature was found on him and because of the passionate poems about a suicide later written by
Gabriela Mistral, a legend was woven around their names. However, it is important to emphasize that this brief episode in Lucila's life was not the sole source of inspiration for her love poetry. The section "Dolor" refers to two different episodes in the
poet's life, but through her manner of writing she purposely lets
the reader believe that the poems are about an only love, frustrated by the suicide of her beloved. This was perhaps her way
of showing that time does not exist and that love is a living
emotion outside of time; or was it perhaps her way of saying to
her second love, who had disappointed her, that she had dismissed him from her thoughts.

From La Cantera in April, 1907, Lucila wrote under the name
of "Alma" for *Penumbras* of La Serena, the paper of David Bari,
which took an avant-garde position in the arts. Lucila also wrote
for *La voz de Elqui* and for *La Reforma.* At that time, too, she
was reading with fervor the works of Rubén Darío, the then
leading poet of Latin America. As she revealed in a letter to her
friend Professor Carlos Soto Ayala, she had been criticized and
had been the victim of many diatribes since she began to write in
1904: "I am proud to inspire attacks and hatred; to inspire con-
tempt would sadden me. I wear an armor which protects me from
any attack brought about by slander and malice: my proud, in-
domitable and unalterable personality. . . . I use the weapons
of indifference and energy to defeat the wretched and I possess
an immense courage to combat the powerful."[31]

Although she had written poetry, Lucila was until that time
known chiefly for her prose. In 1908 the author of *Literatura
Coquimbana,* Carlos Soto Ayala, wrote of her: "The intelligent
prose writer who dips her golden pen in ambrosia."[32]

The year 1910 marked a new phase in Lucila's teaching career
as she rose from the primary-school system to the secondary
school. She was teaching in Barrancas when, encouraged by her
friend Fidelia Valdés and by the poet Víctor Domingo Silva, she
passed very successfully the examination at the Normal School
No. 1 of Santiago, that permitted her to test the knowledge and
skill she had acquired through experience and not through formal
training. The head of that educational institution, Brígida Walker,

immediately understood the sensitivity of the young teacher and offered to let her write in verse the first test, which was in botany. Lucila remained grateful to this educator and dedicated to her memory the beautiful poem "La encina" (The Evergreen Oak) which appeared in *Desolación*.[33] The Reverend Father Medardo Alduan, who met Lucila that year, wrote of her: "I met her in 1910 when she was twenty years old, surrounded by small children, watching over them with motherly fervor. . . . She looked at the children and absorbed humanity. . . . For that reason, she could enter the literary world without any conceit, bearing the name of teacher, . . . and Blanca de los Ríos recognized her work as an apostolate of education, which is the most sublime tribute that we must pay to the Latin American poet."[34]

Thus, Lucila was no longer a romantic adolescent, but a young and dedicated person who had given herself entirely to her vocation as a teacher. She was interested in the development of young minds, anxious to share with them her knowledge, to advise them in their reading, and to guide them on the difficult road of truth, beauty, and hope. The Chilean critic Armando Donoso said of her: "Her purpose was to sow hope and beauty in the hearts of children with the same love as that of a mother who talks to her own flesh and blood."[35] Pablo Neruda, who in 1971 was to win the Nobel Prize for Literature for Latin America, recalled meeting Lucila when he was a young boy, and how she encouraged his avid thirst for reading by offering him some books. He wrote of her: "Gabriela had a radiant smile which disclosed the whiteness of her teeth on her weather-beaten face."[36] Because she could give her love to the children who needed her, she led a rich inner life, yet she was always solitary and withdrawn. She was to say years later: "I have written as someone who speaks in solitude. Because I have been alone everywhere."[37]

In 1911, Lucila taught hygiene at the Public High School of Traiguén for two months, and she was then appointed Head Inspector of Schools and teacher of history at the Public High School for Girls of Antofagasta. According to a critic, she probably owed his position to Teresa Prats Bello, Head Inspector of Primary Education, who had taken an interest in her and had described her thus: "A young lady of noble bearing who has beautiful green eyes with a limpid gaze and princesslike hands."[38] In addition to the time devoted to her absorbing school work, she spent many hours reading and meditating. Among her few friends at Antofagasta were Dr. Pedro Olegario Sánchez, Principal of the Public High School for Boys, and Carlos Parrau Escobar, President of the Lodge "Destellos" affiliated with the Theosophical Society founded in India by Mr. Olcott and Madame Blavatsky. Lucila was fundamentally a Roman Catholic; yet, since she was a mystic always searching for the Eternal, she was attracted for a time to books about the occult. She attended, although with irregularity, some of the meetings of the Lodge held at the home of Dr. Olegario Sánchez. [39]   In December, 1913, and in March, 1914, she wrote for *Nueva Luz,* a magazine connected with the Chilean Theosophical movement, which published her poem "El himno al árbol" (Hymn to the Tree) and her poetic essay "La charca" (The Puddle), both of symbolic and religious significance. Lucila was always to have a deep interest in all religions, but she felt particularly close to some of the concepts of the Orient and for a time believed in reincarnation.

In May, 1912, Lucila was appointed Head Inspector and Professor of history, geography, and Spanish at the Public High School for Girls of Los Andes, where she stayed until 1918 and where she became a well-known literary figure under her pseudonym—Gabriela Mistral. During this period she wrote extensively, as is indicated by the collection of her works which was compiled in 1957 by the eminent Chilean critic Raúl Silva Castro under the title *Producción de Gabriela Mistral de 1912 a 1918.* The book *Epistolario. Cartas a Eugenio Labarca (1915-1916),* also edited by Raúl Silva Castro, gives testimony of her vast correspondence. Lucila lived in the pleasant atmosphere of the city of Los Andes, hemmed in by the Cordillera, and worked under the able guidance of her understanding friend, the principal of the school, Fidelia Valdés Pereira, to whom she dedicated the poem "El encuentro hermoso" (The Beautiful Encounter), published in *Revista de Educación Nacional,* December, 1914. She also wrote of her: "I have taught for six years under the leadership of Fidelia Valdés, the educator whose deep and pure life has given me the brief sparkles of light that my consciousness finds in itself. . . . I have given everything to my profession: my sensitivity, my scant knowledge, my great enthusiasm. I am poor. I only possessed the treasure of my youth and I gave it without a pang. . . ."[40] It was there, too, that she became acquainted with Juana Aguirre de

Aguirre and her husband Pedro Aguirre Cerda, then Minister of Justice and Education and later President of the Republic of Chile (1938-1941). According to José Santos González Vera, Lucila's room looked out on a small patio with an orange tree; a cat, an owl, and a dove became the companions of her solitude.

As was characteristic of her throughout her life, she walked in a straight and rhythmical way, and she dressed with the austere simplicity of a prophet. Lucila did not care for the external adornments of women and, as she was later to write in an article dedicated to the Statue of Liberty, preferred to modern dresses an ancient, long and loose garment, similar to the Roman toga: "I feel a little sting of envy when my eyes fall on it. A bit of frustrated anger overtakes me at having been born at a time of short or long skirts, skirts that are always caricatures and that cannot be compared to the toga. Neither can I resign myself, as I confide to a friend, to not living in some accessible Tunisia or in some India, where I could clad myself in a robe as laden with folds and trailing on the ground as the robe of the Statue of Liberty. . . ."[41] Perhaps influenced by the Orient, she became a vegetarian.

During her years in Los Andes, Lucila became a well-known figure in the literary world. From July to October, 1912, she wrote for the magazine *Sucesos,* published in Valparaíso, and her name appeared as "Gabriela Mistraly," an error due to a misspelling of the pseudonym she was beginning to use. In the same year, she wrote to Rubén Darío, humbly stating how greatly she had been influenced by him and asking him to publish two of her works, if he believed them worthwhile: the poem "El ángel guardián" (The Guardian Angel) and the story "La defensa de la belleza" (In Defense of Beauty), later incorporated in *Desolación* under the title "Por qué las rosas tienen espinas," (Why Roses have Thorns). Her humble letter, signed Lucila Godoy, was written in the then recognized orthography, established in Chile by Andrés Bello. The letter reads as follows:

"Our great and very noble poet: I awaited you at the foot of the Andes to offer you my devotion and that of my children—my pupils—who have been talking about you in a familiar fashion since they read aloud your *'Tale to Margarita'* and your *'Child Rosa.'* But you did not come and I send you in these long pages the pure fragrance that bears the love of a hundred little girls for the poet who writes for them stories like no one ever wrote before.

"Oh, poet: I am a woman and therefore I am fragile, and being a teacher I carry within me something of a doting grandmother. I have given in to the weakness of wanting to write stories and verses for my young ones. And I have written them; I blush as I confess it to you who are as great as you are kind.

"May I dare to ask that you read what I am sending you, namely, a story very much my own and some poems that are completely original.

"May I dare to ask you that if you read them with a benevolent fraternal smile and find somewhere within their core a seed that has something to say, a tiny promise for the future, that you publish them in *Elegancias* or in *Mundial.*

"Rubén, I am unknown; my work has been published in *Sucesos* only for the past two months. I never thought of doing anything else but teach, until the magician that you are, the author of *'Child Rosa',* tempted me and pressed me to do it. You are guilty of so much influence upon the young! If you only knew, if you only knew!"[42]

In March and April, 1913, the works mentioned above were published by Rubén Darío in Paris, in his literary review *Elegancias,* under the name of Gabriela Mistral. This was the first recognition that she received outside of her own country. In her second letter to Rubén Darío (1913), in which she thanked him for publishing her works, she still signed her name "Lucila Godoy," but added her pseudonym "Gabriela Mistral" in parentheses. She wrote:

"Rubén: Should you only find in my story and in my humble verses something hollow, shreds of something common and useless, just write the following word on a sheet of paper: poor, poor and sign it. I am a worshiper of your work and I shall continue to be so.

"Let me explain something: You and Mr. Guido left Mr. Maluenda in charge of selecting material in Chile. This is a fact, but I could not help resisting my spontaneous and holy impulse: to write personally to you Rubén and to receive your straightforward rejection.

"Deeply moved, I take leave of you and I wish upon your noblest of hearts and upon your life an everlasting spring of triumph, you who are the glory of our Latin America.

Humbly yours,
Lucila Godoy
Professor of Spanish at
the Public High School for Girls
Los Andes, 1912

"Do you know Borgues Solar? He has offered to write a prologue to my humble stories."[43]

"Lucila Godoy (Gabriela Mistral) fondly and respectfully greets the great and dear Rubén and is grateful to him for the publication in *Elegancias* of her story and her verses. She encloses something still unpublished should it please him to retain it for publication.

"My good wishes, oh Poet, for your health and everlasting spiritual blossoming.

(Chile) Los Andes, 1913"[44]

She continued to use her pen name throughout her life, and it became known all over the world. Yet, for some years she used her pseudonym interchangeably with her real name, "Lucila Godoy," as is seen in her poem "El himno cotidiano" (The Daily Hymn), published in *Revista de Educación Nacional*, July, 1913, and in her correspondence with her friends. Sometimes she also signed her works "Gab. Mistral." During the latter part of 1913 and during 1914, her works appeared mainly under her pseudonym as shown in *Norte y Sur,* Santiago, No. 2, September, 1913; *Sucesos,* Valparaíso, October 23, 1913, and February 5, March 5, March 23, April 23, 1914; *Nueva Luz,* Santiago, December, 1913, and March, 1914; and *Revista de Educación Nacional,* March and December, 1914. Thus, it may be said that in the years 1913 and 1914, Lucila Godoy established herself as "Gabriela Mistral."

The name "Gabriela Mistral" really became recognized on December 22, 1914, when, during the celebration of the Floral Games in the Teatro Santiago, she was awarded the highest distinction. This was a poetry contest organized in Santiago by the Society of Artists and Writers of Chile in which four hundred works competed. In an effort to rejuvenate poetry, an appeal had been made to the young writers of Chile and in response the humble teacher of Los Andes submitted her contributions. Serving on the jury were the poet Manuel Magallanes Moure, who presided, and Armando Donoso, and Miguel Luis Rocuant. Although Miguel Luis Rocuant favored the poem "Plegaria a María" (Prayer to Mary) by Julio Munizaga Ossandón, Gabriela Mistral's "Los sonetos de la muerte" (Sonnets on Death) were received with great warmth. The Sonnets were three in number. They created a new and distinct tone in their passionate, violent, and intimate qualities. There is reason to believe that these sonnets were first written in 1909, the year of the death of Romelio Ureta, for when they were published in the magazine *Zig-Zag,* on March 6, 1915, the year 1909 appeared at the bottom of the page, indicating that the poet had purposely not wanted to publish them immediately. One may also presume that Gabriela Mistral wrote a series of "Sonetos de la Muerte," of which only six are known; three praised in the Floral Games, later included in *Desolación,* two published in the anthology *Selva Lírica* (Lyrical Poems), in 1917, and never reprinted in her own books, and one which appeared as "De los sonetos de la muerte" (From the Sonnets on Death), followed by the Roman Number XI, first published in *Primrose* (Chillán), No. 38, August 1, 1915, and incorporated in *Desolación* under the title of "La condena" (The Sentence). These sonnets in which she revealed a metaphysical and stirring familiarity with death crowned her success.

Yet, because of her modesty, Gabriela Mistral did not take part in the honor that was bestowed upon her and was said to have viewed the ceremony of the Floral Games from the gallery, unknown to all: "A legend woven by rumor tells that she did not attend the ceremony to read her poems because she did not have the proper attire to fit the occasion, and that she witnessed her own triumph from the top gallery."[45] It was her friend, the poet Víctor Domingo Silva, who recited her poetry, spoke of her activities as a teacher, her excessive modesty of character, and who compared her to the Italian poet and educator Ada Negri.[46]

Much has been said of the pseudonym of Gabriela Mistral and of the influences that made her choose it. The Cuban critic Jorge Mañach gave it the following definition: "Gabriela: Soul and Earth"; Virgilio Figueroa, who wrote her first biography, says of her name: "*Gabriela* represents the presence of the spirit, *Mistral* the breeze of the earth." It is generally believed that "Gabriela" meant for her, as said above, the prophetic spirit of the archangel who brought a message of life; "Mistral," the love that she bore nature in the evocation of the Mediterranean wind, lively and powerful, together with her great admiration for the Provençal poet Frédéric Mistral. During these years she became acquainted with the works of Frédéric Mistral and was to dedicate to his *Mireille* two poems: "Del libro de Mireya" (From the book of Mireille) and "La plegaria" (The Prayer), published in *Sucesos,* April 27 and May 4, 1916, respectively. In a letter written to her young friend Eugenio Labarca some time in 1915-1916, she also mentioned her admiration for the Provencal poet and affectionately referred to him as "My great old friend Mistral."[47] In her poem "Mis libros" (My Books), published in *Desolación,* she praised some of the books and writers that had influenced her life: the Bible, St. Francis of Assisi, Amado Nervo, and Frédéric Mistral's *Mireille:*

> *Oh Poem of Mistral, that has the fragrance*
> *of an open furrow in the mountains,*
> *I draw you in, enraptured!*
> *I saw Mireille press the fruit*
> *bathed in the crimson color of love*
> *and run through the enormous desert.*[48]

Gabriela later in her life gave this explanation of her pseudonym during an interview with *Les Lettres Françaises:* "I wanted a pseudonym that would evoke the force of nature that I like the most: the wind. But, she adds quickly, I also found an intellectual bond with your poet."[49] It is interesting to note that she signed her name "Gabrielamistral" as if it consisted of one word, eliminating the capital letter in Mistral. This perhaps meant that she considered her pen name as a unit and placed an equal stress on the two forces she had found in her name.

Following the award in the poetry contest, many visitors came to Los Andes to see Gabriela Mistral, and prominent persons in the literary world corresponded with her. The principal writers of Latin America—the Mexicans Amado Nervo, Enrique González Martínez, José Vasconcelos, and many others—became interested in her work. Amado Nervo, in his understanding of her suffering and her struggles, used the word "Sister" in speaking of the young Chilean and considered her one of the great poets of modern times.[50] The letters of Gabriela Mistral relating to this period of her life reveal the spontaneity of her nature and her constant desire to be of help. She thought of herself as a "teacher" and in her humble way felt responsible for the minds of the younger generation, as if her mission were to guide each of them into a spiritual and idealistic world. She wrote in a letter to Eugenio Labarca: ". . . I have a pursuit. I believe that I have a mission on this morsel of earth to free from philosophical materialism those few who some day will play an important part in the world of arts and education. This is the reason why I have a tendency to preach. Do not laugh; and accept the humble role that I play at your side."[51] She felt close to religious men and for a long time she contemplated writing about the unknown saints of the world, to whom she later devoted some beautiful articles and poems: "I have been thinking about this for a long time, to write a eulogy of the highest unknown spirits who are the salt of the earth and the light of the world as the parable says."[52]

Gabriela's thoughts were constantly concerned with the literary world of Chile and its development of spiritual values. She shared with her friends her thoughts on writers in whom she found spiritual elements close to her own. She could only admire a literary work that had profound ideas, for to her the best friend of beauty was truth, and mind was the highest muse.[53] She once wrote: "I love beauty and I kneel besides it wherever it may be."[54] Some of the writers she mentioned at that time were: Delmira Agustini, María Monvel, Juanita Quindos, Eugenia Vaz-Ferreira, Alone (Hernán Díaz Arrieta), Azorín, Darío, Dostoevski, Emerson, Gorky, Guerra Junqueiro, Juan Ramón Jiménez, Maeterlinck, Amado Nervo, Pedro Prado, Romain Rolland, Shakespeare, Rabindranath Tagore, Tolstoy, Turgenev, Unamuno, and Augusto Winter.

Gabriela rarely wrote about her own works. However, according to information which she gave to Eugenio Labarca, she planned to write a volume of poetry for children called *Versos escolares* (Poems for Schoolchildren). Labarca's article about her was published in *Primrose* (Chillán), February 21, 1915. She wanted to create a new style of poetry for children, which would be artistic and impregnated with the living breath of God: "I wish to write a new kind of poetry for schoolchildren because the poems that are popular today do not satisfy me. I wish to write verses that will not be deprived of poetry even though they are written for school purposes. On the contrary, I want these poems to be more delicate than any others, deeper, more filled with the things of the heart, quivering with the inner breath of the soul."[55]

She thought also of publishing a second book in the genre of "Los sonetos de la muerte", but it appeared as her first, under the title *Desolación*.

The elements that emanate from her letters are her sincerity and her independent character. In four of her letters she wrote:

"As one who teaches children, I am sincere."[56]

"It was a question of speaking the truth and, for a good reason, I am a teacher of children."[57]

"When one says one's truth, one feels a sense of delight and deep satisfaction."[58]

"If there is any worth in me, it is not my humble poetry or my prose, but it is my baffling sincerity, my loyalty toward my own people, my incapacity to hurt anyone."[59]

As she said in a letter to Nataniel Yáñez Silva in which she defended the literary group "The Ten," she was independent of all groups, or in her own words: "I am an outsider."[60] Thus Gabriela created her own style. She shunned large assemblies of people and sometimes wished she could have remained the unknown Lucia Godoy: "I almost always keep away from success and come near those who begin."[61] She fled from praise and, as she beautifully expressed it, preferred to it the simple and sincere expression of friendship: "I would like to tell you that I have very little or no liking for public praise. I enjoy more the loyal letter of a man or woman with a refined spirit than daily articles that praise with exaggeration."[62] Although she was only twenty-six years old at that time, she felt, as already appears in her letter to Rubén Darío in 1912, like an old woman whose aim in life was to educate and to guide the young. She often said of herself: "I am old and would like to give you some advice. Forgive me for the sermon. This is what we the old are for."[63] She called herself: "An affectionate grandmother to young artists."

After Gabriela Mistral was crowned in the Floral Games, her name crossed the boundaries of Chile and her poetry and her prose appeared in numerous literary reviews, sometimes even without her consent or knowledge. This fact is important because, as Gabriela Mistral corrected her work constantly until she arrived at a final draft acceptable to herself, she was unhappy to see in print some of her poetry in a form she no longer cared for. Throughout her life, she had this need for correcting her writings, and carried it to such an extent that she even made changes, minor as well as fundamental, in poems that had already been published for more than twenty years.

Although her name appeared in such Chilean literary reviews as *Pacífico Magazine, Figulinas, Sucesos, Primrose* (Chillán), *Luz y Sombra, Familia, Ideales* (Concepción), *La Sombra Inquieta, Zig-Zag, Los Diez,* and magazines and newspapers of the American continent reproduced her songs, she continued to live humbly in the small town of Los Andes. Her father had died in 1915, and since "Los sonetos de la muerte" she was constantly preoccupied by thoughts of death and of the life beyond. Isaura Dinator de Guzmán upon meeting Gabriela Mistral, who had come to Santiago on a short visit, was impressed by her simple attire and yet her majestic mien and her conversation in which she revealed her great love of children. She gave of Gabriela the following description: "She appeared to me as a beautiful young woman radiant with youth, who had extremely handsome green eyes. Her complexion was fair and her features were graceful."[64] Much has been said of her bearing: the aristocratic slenderness of her hands, the beauty of her eyes, and the disarming quality of her warm and generous smile. Isaura's husband, Manuel Guzmán Maturana, an educator and a writer, whose home was an educational and literary center, immediately recognized Gabriela's greatness. He urged her to write some poems and prose pieces for his five-volume series of textbooks. Although at first she refused because she did not feel prepared, fifty-five selections of her poems and prose were included in Guzmán Maturana's *Libros de Lecturas* (Books of Selected Readings), between 1916 and 1918. These books were used in various countries of Latin America and contributed to her fame inside and outside of Chile. Three of her commentaries in prose and three in verse were also included in Raúl Ramírez's book *Rabindranath Tagore, poeta y filósofo hindú* (Rabindranath Tagore, Hindu Poet and Philosopher), published in Santiago in 1917, and nine of her poems were published in the anthology *Selva Lírica,* compiled by Juan Agustín Araya and Julio Molina Núñez, and issued in Santiago in 1917.

Despite this growing fame, Gabriela found moments of peace in her daily work with the young and in her writings: "I want to get my strength back to accomplish my task, for it is my only reason for living. I have given myself to children and only for them do I keep my health and impetus. I am an old maid in love with other people's children."[65] Her letters to Eugenio Labarca and to others, as well as her writings, stand as a record of that period of her life. She hardly left the town of Los Andes, except for a few trips to Santiago and probably one to Concepción, as indicated by her poem "Pinares" (Pine Groves), published in *Ideales,* Concepción, in July, 1915, with the notation "Pinares de Concepción" written at the end of the poem. It is thus possible to say that what inspired her work at that time was the natural beauty of Los Andes and its vicinity. She called it "Tierra nevada" (Land of Snow) in the note that follows her poetic and idealistic essay "El picacho" (The Peak), published in *Sucesos,* July 29, 1915. Because she later lived in Punta Arenas, Magallanes, in the antarctic region, many people have erroneously believed that the term "Tierra nevada" referred to that southernmost point of Chile with which she was not as yet acquainted.

Characteristically, Gabriela preferred leading a quiet life in Los Andes to being embroiled in the crowds and the noise of a large city. Santiago attracted her with its theatres, its public library, and its many bookstores. It should be recalled that she read with vehement passion and that her first visit in any city was to a bookstore. If there were no new books available, she would buy those that she·had already read, just for the pleasure of having them in her hands: "She reads as if it were prescribed by a doctor. She jots down the essential in a note book. . . . and if she does not find new books, she acquires works that she knows by heart only to have the pleasure of leafing through them. It is a sedative for her nerves—the nerves of a prophet. She later offers the books to her young protégés."[66] She disliked city life because she could only feel happy as a part of nature. She had a need for peace and quiet, for trees and flowers. Throughout her life, wherever she went, she chose to live in the country, and would select a house, not for its own sake but because its garden appealed to her: "To live happily I need to have a large stretch of heaven and trees, much sky and many trees."[67] Gabriela Mistral lived in Los Andes until 1918 under the protection of Fidelia Valdés whom she called her sister. For the next four years, she served as principal in the various secondary schools of Chile. It was during these travels in her youth that she studied and recorded with a careful and loving eye the people, the flora, and the fauna of her country, and learned its geography at first hand. She later depicted these impressions poetically in her writings. Her posthumous work *Poema de Chile* (Poem about Chile) stands out as a vivid expression of her abiding love for Chile.

Through the help of her friend Pedro Aguirre Cerda, who admired her poetry and her work as an educator, Gabriela Mistral was appointed in 1918 principal of the Public High School for Girls of Punta Arenas, now known as Magallanes. It was probably in that city that she developed her great love for Patagonia, the southernmost land of America, or as she called it: "The land where the world ends." Later, she would often speak of the experience of seeing the midnight sun. She would recall with affection that frigid and wind-ridden region, its dense forests and its warm and friendly people: "I have traveled through the most beloved region of my land, through Patagonia. Near the Antarctic, the climate is rough, it is very cold, but the people are very warm and kind. I always remember this land with fondness in spite of the fact that it is there that I acquired this tremendous rheumatism that comes back every year."[68]

The sculptress Laura Rodig, who had known Gabriela in Los Andes and who had gone with her to her new post, was impressed by the contributions of the young poet and teacher to every social undertaking. Gabriela had known and loved the humble and defenseless and could never abandon them. She visited prisons and hospitals, and gave personal help, material and spiritual, to young children, especially those suffering from malnutrition and rickets. She once said: "I want to give myself completely to the teaching of the poor."[69] Today, trees planted by her on Avenida Colón and on the Plaza de Punta Arenas stand tall and strong as a mark of her short but loving sojourn there. Every place in which Gabriela Mistral lived influenced her, and she, in turn, left on it the mark of her personality. As she had been moved by the precipitous landscape of Los Andes, its mountains and its river, she was also stirred by every detail of the southernmost portion of Latin America. Laura Rodig recalls that Gabriela put down all her impressions in little notebooks. Some of the titles—"Los pájaros de Chile" (Birds of Chile), "Las mariposas" (Butterflies), "El Folklore" (Folklore), "Yerbas medicinales" (Medicinal Herbs)— give added proof of her deep-rooted interest in nature.[70] A large part of *Desolación* was written in Punta Arenas. Perhaps it was the small island of Desolación close by that inspired the title of her book.

Pacífico Magazine of Santiago published "El niño solo" (The Lonely Child) in September, 1919, and her article "Al pueblo hebreo" (To the Hebrew People) appeared in *Renacimiento,* a Jewish magazine in Santiago, in November, 1919. "El pensador de Rodin" (Rodin's Thinker) was published by Cervantes of Madrid in January, 1920, and "Cristina Soro" in August, 1920. This firm had been publishing her works since 1917.[71]

In 1920, Gabriela Mistral was appointed principal and professor of Spanish at the Public High School of Temuco, which she reorganized. It was there that she was inspired to write "Poemas de la madre más triste" (Poems of the Saddest of Mothers), when in a poor neighborhood she saw an expectant mother cringe as a passerby made a coarse remark. Gabriela had a feeling of solidarity with her sex and believed that it was her mission to reveal the true meaning and sanctity of motherhood, even if she should be criticized:

"Since men have not written about it, it is up to us, women, to tell about the sanctity of this painful and divine state. If the purpose of art is to embellish everything, in an all-embracing compassion, why have we not purified this state to the eyes of the unholy?

"[My poems] are dedicated to those women who are capable of seeing that the sanctity of life begins in motherhood, which is therefore holy. May they feel the deep tenderness with which the woman who fosters the children of others looks at the mothers of all the children of the world."[72]

Laura Rodig recalled their trip on Rio Imperial and their one-day stay in Puerto Saavedra and Lago Budy as hosts of the poet

Augusto Winter. It was also in Temuco that they met Pablo Neruda: "And they were both bound by the same tie, a symbolic alliance. Geography and soul of Chile that rise over the world, like a never ending melody sung in two voices."[73]

In February, 1921, Federico de Onís, professor of Spanish literature at Columbia University and director of the Hispanic Institute in the United States, gave a lecture there on Gabriela Mistral to an audience composed chiefly of teachers and students of Spanish who had never heard her name. They were all so impressed by the beauty of her poetry and by its moral loftiness that they wanted to know more about their South American sister, who was, like them, a teacher. From this lecture sprang the idea of publishing her first book, *Desolación,* under the auspices of the Institute.

In the same year, Gabriela was transferred to Santiago as the first principal of Public High School No. 6, founded in May, 1920. This was the highest position in the secondary-school system. For this school she composed eighteen maxims which reveal the purity of the rules of conduct that she felt should guide teachers and her religious and missionary-like concept of teaching. These are a few of her precepts:

"1. Everything for the school; very little for ourselves.
  2. To teach always: in the courtyard and in the street as well as in the classroom. To teach with one's bearing, one's actions, and one's words.

. . . .

  5. It is necessary to live up to one's position each day. To be occasionally skillful is not enough.
  6. One should not be afraid to correct. The worst teacher is he who knows fear.
  7. Everything can be said; but the right words should be sought. The most severe reprimand can be made without humiliating and poisoning the soul.
  8. The teaching of children is perhaps the highest form of seeking God; but it is also the most frightening because of its tremendous responsibility.
  9. It is as dangerous for the superficial teacher to chat with her pupil as it is beautiful for the teacher who has some-

thing to offer her pupil to continue her lesson outside of the classroom.

. . . .

17. Beauty can be found in every lesson.
18. There is nothing sadder than for the student to realize that the class lecture is the equivalent of his text book."[74]

Gabriela put her trust and her hope in children, for she believed that through them the world could become purer: "Children continue being the expression of my faith in a better and more just world than ours."[75] In June, 1921, while in Santiago, her "Poemas de las madres" (Poems about Mothers), a religious explanation of maternity, were published in *Repertorio Americano* of San José, Costa Rica. She once said about these poems, written in poetic prose:" . . . They are almost unpublished since they appeared in a journal that only circulates among teachers: the *Revista de Educación Nacional.* They were later published successfully in Buenos Aires. I was afraid and I still am that they may frighten the prudes, because even though my writings are pure, they are realistic."[76]

While she was principal of Public High School No. 6 (in 1921), a law was passed that prohibited the appointment of teachers without university degrees, and Gabriela resigned. It was at this time that José Vasconcelos, Secretary of Public Education of Mexico, who had represented his country at the commemoration of Brazilian independence, visited Chile on his way home. He met Gabriela and after a long interview asked her to come to Mexico to assist him in educational reforms.

CHAPTER 2

Cultural
and
Diplomatic
Activities
in Other
Countries

> *"I am a wandering Chilean who has
> partaken of the fraternal bread
> of three continents, receiving
> from them, day after day, the
> full benefit of their culture."*
>
> GABRIELA MISTRAL

GABRIELA MISTRAL traveled throughout Chile, from the north to the extreme south; she covered the whole length of her country and retained in her heart all of its elements. Her wanderings had their roots in the life of her forebears, but they were also part of her mission as an apostle, and one of the sources of her maturity. The first stage of her journey was Chile, the second was Mexico. It was from there that she first saw her country in perspective and that she first embraced in her concern all the problems of Latin America.

In June, 1922, a new career began for Gabriela as she left Chile for the first time. She had been invited by the Mexican Government under President Obregón to collaborate in educational reform at a time when the country was experiencing a spiritual and aesthetic rebirth. Mexico's beloved poets, González Martínez and María Enriqueta, were both friends of Gabriela Mistral. Soon after her arrival she met Palma Guillén, who was to accompany her during her stay in Mexico and to be like a sister to her for the rest of her life: ". . . We worked together and we had the close relationship of two people who see each other every day and who, little by little, get to know each other and build a true friendship . . ."[1] Palma later married Luis Nicolau d'Olwer, a writer and high official at the time of the Spanish Republic.

This trip was the beginning of Gabriela's pilgrimage through the three Americas and Europe. She set out from Valparaíso on board the "Aconcagua" bound for Veracruz, passing through the Panama Canal. In Havana she was greeted by a group of poets and journalists, and in Mexico she received the highest homage ever given to Chile. Poets surrounded her at a luncheon in Chapultepec Park, children sang her "rondas"[2] put to music, and she was offered the key of every city. José Vasconcelos greeted her thus:

"Because these days there is no woman more admired and loved than you, Gabriela, because you are the living radiance that uncovers the secrets of the soul and the destinies of nations. . . .

"From now on, we Mexicans have been enriched with one more day of glory. We feel pride and joy to have you in our midst, to know that you love us and wish us well. We have stretched our arms so many times toward the South seeking a friendship weakened by distance!

"You have finally come, the highest of emissaries, with a heart that goes beyond its boundaries in search of twenty scattered nations to bind them in a sole, loving embrace."[3]

Pedro Prado, the Chilean author, had written these words to the Mexican people:

"You will see her come and she will awaken in you the secret melancholy that unknown vessels bring forth as they reach the port.

"She will come, her hair combed back, with a calm gait, moving with a gentle and majestic rhythm. She is like a ship covered with dew drops that comes from the depth of the night to emerge with the dawn bringing to the harbor deep in sleep the light of a new day.

"Do not flutter about her for she wages a battle for simplicity."[4]

Gabriela herself wrote about the importance of remaining unaffected and of her endeavor to avoid an elaborate style: "I have greatly struggled to achieve an elemental simplicity."[5] In spite of her dislike for publicity, many schools, libraries, and streets were named after her, and it was in Mexico that the first statue was erected to her. She had been invited to Mexico for six months, but her stay was extended for two years—from 1922 to 1924. At first she lived in the Hotel Genève and then in a beautiful country house in San Angel, today Villa Obregón, a suburb of Mexico

City. From there she transmitted her teachings to the whole South American continent, and there she wrote her beautiful pieces on the countryside and the people of Mexico. She worked under José Vasconcelos in reforming the school system, raising the moral standard of the Indian, and redeeming him from poverty through a new kind of primary education in which he could learn trades and crafts. As she had dedicated herself to the children of Chile, so did she give herself to the cause of the Indian, crossing the Mexican Plateau on horseback and reaching the most inaccessible villages. In those remote places Gabriela gathered together the rural teachers and explained to them the way to teach Spanish and history.[6] She personally organized outdoor schools with three or four teachers who went directly to teach the Indians:

"My continuous and meticulous travels through the countryside of many Mexican states were not 'pleasure trips to enjoy the landscape' as some teachers have said, but a series of personal interviews with teachers from the cities and teachers from villages, in Puebla, Michoacán, etc. The school inspectors from these regions have officially acknowledged my work and I hold in my possession these clear and conclusive documents. I did not want to publish them in order not to take on a polemic attitude which I find quite unpleasant regarding a country to which I am deeply indebted and that possesses the highest moral standards."[7]

Perhaps it was in Mexico that she learned to love and to know the native cultures of America. On her frequent trips to small villages she lived among Indians, shared their lives, and spoke to them with religious emotion. She was always animated by love and worked with energy, and she became the mother of all poor and abandoned children. She liked to hear their languages and their expressions. Perhaps, too, she understood them so well because she thought of herself, although with exaggeration, as an Indian; she possessed their melancholy and the touch of humility. She once said: "I am reserved to the point of humility and proud to the point of haughtiness."[8] It seemed that, like José Martí, the Cuban poet and liberator, whom she greatly admired, Gabriela Mistral achieved, from contact with the Mexican soil, an all-embracing love for humanity. José Martí was one of the voices that had molded her. Gabriela absorbed and sang the beauty of Mexico, its atmosphere of reform, and its revolutionary spirit. She was an antimilitarist who fought for justice and equality for all men. In a lecture, she said of the Indian:

"Different is his home from mine, different his prayer. It does not matter! He was bathed in the same light of revelation at the moment of creation. I knew then that we were equal, not because of 'the mercy found in the Christian commandments, nor in so-called civic equality, but because of the essence of our very being, that is to say, completely."[9]

In her beautiful poem "Beber" (Drinking) she revealed once again her fraternal love for him:

> *In the countryside of Mitla,*
> *by a scorching sun, with locusts and fatigue,*
> *I bent over a well*
> *and an Indian came to hold me over the water,*
> *and my head, like a fruit,*
> *was between his palms.*
> *I was drinking what he drank,*
> *which was his face with mine,*
> *and in a flash I knew*
> *that his race and mine were one.*[10]

I recall with what affection she spoke of Mexican Indians; to her, the Indian was a magnet that she carried within her heart.[11] Laura Rodig recounts what happened at a convention of delegates of Mexican farmers held in the amphitheater of the university which Gabriela attended incognito. A peasant recognized her and knelt in front of her. Gabriela took his hands in hers and in her simple and fraternal way kissed them in front of a thousand persons gathered there:

"Suddenly we saw the man fall to his knees and Gabriela came close to him and took between her luminous hands his dark hands, the weather-beaten roots of the peasant who toils with the earth, and in an act of anointing she kissed them. This reverential gesture had a deep symbolic meaning and was felt by those present as their eyes grew moist."[12]

It was in Mexico, with its profound traces of Spanish culture, that she learned to love and respect Spain. It was also there that she lived without economic stress and with a sensation of peace. She admired the simplicity of the Mexican people and among them she did not feel that she was a stranger:

"Absolute and outgoing simplicity is a Mexican quality which warms my heart. Their spirit has won me over. And here I am walking the streets with a feeling of ease as someone who walks in his own yard. I will tell you what has impressed me the most. I arrived at the home they had prepared for me in the country. I went to the rooftop. The horizon was boundless and I felt the embrace of the light directly descending from heaven and the silent embrace of all the fields that were all about me. For the first time in eighteen years I knew that I could work in peace, without the call of the school bell at the strike of each new hour, without the economic anguish that upsets my life continuously. I praised God and blessed with all my heart that foreign land that was granting me such peace."[13]

A high point in Gabriela's stay in Mexico was the publication of her first two books: *Desolación* and *Lecturas para mujeres* (Selected Readings for Women). In San Angel she prepared the collection of her poems and prose that she sent to Federico de Onís in New York after she had met him personally in Mexico in 1922. With her usual modesty she would not have collected them had she not been pressed to do so by Onís. The Hispanic Institute in the United States, founded by him at Columbia University in 1920, published her first book, *Desolación,* in 1922. The first edition carried the following statement: "Edition dedicated to the author by the teachers of Spanish, in testimony of their admiration and affection." Gabriela dedicated her book to Pedro Aguirre Cerda and his wife Juana Aguirre de Aguirre to whom, as she said, "she owed the hour of peace" in which she lived. The appendix consisted of a vow in which Gabriela Mistral promised never again to write a bitter book, but to sing words of hope to console every creature. She had written these poems to relieve her tragic past:

"May God forgive me for writing this bitter book and may those men and women who see life as something gentle, also forgive me.

"In these hundred poems there bleeds a painful past, a past in which my songs became stained with blood to mitigate my sorrow. I leave it behind me like a somber lowland and climb unto a more clement hillside to reach the spiritual plateaus where an all-embracing light will fall upon my days. I will sing from their heights, praising hope, without ever looking into my grieving heart; I will use my songs as a compassionate soul said: 'to console men.' When I was thirty, I wrote the 'Decalogue of the Artist' and I made this vow.

"May God and may life allow me to fulfill this promise in the days that are left to me on my life's journey . . ."[14]

She had known solitude and suffering, but her pessimism had been creative. Her name which, until then, had been known only through literary magazines, newspapers, and schoolbooks, became popular throughout the Americas. However, she could not keep this promise. Although for a time her poems were serene, her personal sorrow in her last journey through life made her songs erupt into passionate and bitter poems that recall the emotion of her early years.

A second edition of *Desolación* appeared in 1923 in Santiago, Chile, with a poetic prologue by Pedro Prado. In the same year Gabriela, urged by José Vasconcelos, completed an anthology of the poetry and prose of various authors, including some of her material both published and unpublished. This book, whose complete title was *Lecturas para mujeres destinadas a la enseñanza del lenguaje* (Readings for Women Selected for the Purpose of Teaching the Language) was published in Mexico in 1923 under the auspices of the Ministry of Education. Twenty thousand copies were printed. During the dedication of the school "Escuela-Hogar Gabriela Mistral," for which she had compiled the book, she was accompanied to the lecture platform by the poets Jaime Torres Bodet and Rafael Heliodoro Valle. The topic of her speech was: "The gift of souls."[15] She said: "I will always feel a sense of pride that gives rise to serenity at having received from the hands of Dr. José Vasconcelos the gift of a school in Mexico, and the opportunity to write a book for the women of Latin America in the only time of rest that I have known in my life."[16]

Gabriela first went to the United States in 1924 where she was honored on May 13 at the Pan American Union in Washington. Mrs. H. A. Coleman, one of the speakers and President of the National League of Women Writers of the United States, spoke of Gabriela Mistral whose life was dedicated to the welfare of humanity through work with children and whose destiny had designated her as an apostle of truth. Gabriela, in turn, spoke of the equality of the Indian, of the role of the United States, and of religion. She said that among the men who had formed her character was Emerson, "a tonic, fortifying like the air one breathes in a pine grove and that lights up the dark mines of the human soul."[17]

Gabriela became at that time a contributor to the magazine *Nueva Democracia* of New York. In it, she published many articles on religion, the relationship of the United States with South American countries, and other topics. Later in 1924 she took her first trip to Europe. She visited France, Italy, Switzerland, and Spain. Some beautiful articles stand as a reminder of that period of her life; her interview with Giovanni Papini, her descriptions of the Mediterranean, Naples, Siena, Florence, Majorca, and Castile. Her second book of poetry, *Ternura* (Tenderness), was published by Editorial Calleja in Madrid in 1924. At a reception in her honor offered by the P.E.N. Club of Madrid, the Spanish critic Enrique Diez Canedo spoke of her austere grace and of the universal fraternity that illumined her work.

In February, 1925, Gabriela Mistral left Europe for Chile. The return trip to Latin America was a triumphant one; she was received with enthusiasm in Brazil, Uruguay, Argentina, and in her own country where she remained a few months. On March 4, 1925, she was granted a pension for her work as a teacher. From 1905 on, she had taken every step in the teaching profession; though she had obtained her teaching certificate without having attended any Normal School (a Teacher's College), she received an honorary diploma from the University of Chile. José Maza, the Minister of Education, said of her at a parliamentary session: ". . . Gabriela Mistral has achieved a literary production of exceptional importance for Chilean culture. Through her patriotic work, Spanish letters are indebted to the spirit of Chile."[18]

Gabriela with her usual simplicity wished to remain in Chile and to become once more a rural school teacher. However, her desire to live among her people in the Valley of Elqui, to have a little school of her own and raise some goats, was not granted. Beginning in 1926 she continued the roving life she had begun in 1922. The Chilean Government appointed her its representative in the International Institute of Intellectual Cooperation, an organization connected with the League of Nations with headquarters in the Palais Royal in Paris. The Institute's first Director,

Julien Luchaire, wrote to the Argentine poet Leopoldo Lugones about the nomination of Gabriela Mistral as "Head of the Literary Section": ". . . The Spanish language is thus represented at the International Institute by one of those who use it most productively."[19] Gabriela also became adviser for South American affairs.[20]

In the same year, 1925, she visited Argentina where the third edition of *Desolación* was published by Editorial Nascimento with a foreword by the Chilean critic Alone (Hernán Díaz Arrieta) in addition to the prologue by Pedro Prado, which had first appeared in the second edition. The Argentine writer Alberto Gerchunoff wrote of her: "She seemed like a farm girl who had just come to the city and who in the midst of all the turmoil had kept the free, flowing manner of the peasant who sows. She was like a saint, as saints should be in their pious strivings."[21] It was in 1925 that she met Romain Rolland in Switzerland and wrote an article about him in *El Mercurio* of Santiago.

During 1926, 1927, and part of 1928, Gabriela traveled in France, Italy, and Switzerland, wherever her work took her, accompanied by her friend Palma Guillén. In a letter dated January 7, 1927, she wrote to the Director Julien Luchaire that she was preparing a complete documentation on Latin America. In February, 1927, she lived in a small country house in Fontainebleau, for as always she fled large cities. In February 1927, she succeeded Joaquín Edwards-Bello as Chilean Delegate to the International Institute of Intellectual Cooperation. She went to Provence, the land from which she had taken the name "Mistral," in May, 1927, and from there she continued to further the works of the Institute by preparing reports about Latin America. During that year she also represented the Teachers Association of Chile at the Congress of Educators at Locarno and attended the Congress of Children's Welfare held in Geneva. Her letters to Benjamín Carrión reveal her constant interest in Spanish America and her admiration for many of its writers. Because of her love of books and her desire to guide her friends, she recommended the books of writers she considered important; among them: Arturo Capdevila (Argentina), Pedro Prado, Martha Brunet, Torres Rioseco, and Pablo Neruda (Chile)—she wrote of Pablo Neruda: "He is our best writer in contemporary poetry"—[22], Jorge Mañach (Cuba), Arévalo Martínez (Guatemala)— "He is, without doubt, the first-rate writer from Central America"—[23], Xavier Villaurrutia, Carlos Pellicer, and Torres Bodet (Mexico), Carlos Sabat Ercasty, Juana de Ibarbourou, and Carlos Vaz Ferreira (Uruguay), Teresa de la Parra (Venezuela). She devoted much of her time to the works of philosophers, biographers, and poets, and was less interested in novels. She kept up with Latin American literature and current events. From Pertuis in Vaucluse, she wrote in August, 1927: "My health has much improved. The joy of the sun and the sea has penetrated me; I am in a good mood, anxious to read and write." [24]

During 1927, she founded, with the Peruvian writer and diplomat Víctor Andrés Belaúnde, then technical adviser to the Institute, the Collection of Ibero-American Classics within the International Institute of Intellectual Cooperation. This undertaking was under the direction of a Publication Committee formed after the meeting of the Latin American Delegates on March 15, 1927. The Committee was presided over by the delegate of Switzerland, Gonzague de Reynold, and its first Secretary General was Giuseppe Prezzolini, who later was succeeded by Dominique Braga. The Collection, today continued by UNESCO, was designed to acquaint the French-speaking public with the principal authors of Latin America through translations of the most representative works of Latin American writers that best reflected America, its folklore, and its culture. The Committee at first wanted to publish the works of Latin American writers in French, Italian, English, and German translations. Gabriela was so interested in this plan that she would have published the four editions at her own expense if she had had the means. For lack of funds, the collection was published only in French.

From France, Italy, Spain, the United States, and the Latin American countries in which she traveled and lived from 1927 to 1938, Gabriela worked generously for the Collection of Ibero-American Classics. Dominique Braga said to me that she not only contributed to the Collection, but had been its very soul. She prepared lists of books, which were approved by the delegates of the Latin American countries, and she proposed the translations of the works of such writers as Eugenio María Hostos, José Martí, and Rubén Darío. She said: "Darío's volume must spring forth from the collaboration of the whole Latin American continent."[25] She corresponded with many people all over Latin America to find subsidies for new volumes. Thus, through her devoted help, Argentina voted to finance four volumes in May, 1928; Chile financed two volumes in October, 1928; Brazil paid for four volumes in April, 1929; and Venezuela, four volumes in June, 1930. At her suggestion, the two Chilean volumes were published under the titles of *Historiens chiliens* (Chilean Historians), 1930, and *Folklore chilien* (Chilean Folklore), 1938. Although she knew nothing about the management of money in her private life, she was active in finding the necessary subsidies in Colombia, Cuba, and Puerto Rico for the furthering of the Collection. She wrote in a letter: "As always I am at your disposal for the raising of money."[26] Through her efforts she made better known in Europe the intellectual world of Latin America and she contributed in Latin America to a better knowledge of the work done by the Institute and the League of Nations. She published an article on the work of the Institute in *El Mercurio,* Santiago, Chile, on March 13, 1927.

Some of the translators who made the work of the Collection possible were: Mathilde Pomès, Charles Auburn, Marcel Bataillon, Roger Caillois, who was to become Director of the Collection of Representative Works published by UNESCO and in 1971 Member of the French Academy; Marcel Carayon, Jean Cassou, Max Daireaux, Francis de Miomandre, Georges Pillement, Georgette and Jacques Soustelle—all hispanists.

During her work at the Institute, from 1927 to 1938, Gabriela met Henri Bergson, whom she greatly admired, Madame Curie, Paul Claudel, Georges Duhamel, and Paul Valéry. She also knew Francois Mauriac and Georges Bernanos, whom she met in 1929 in Vichy.

In 1927-1928, as well as throughout the next decade, many Latin American writers were gathered in Paris. Among some of them were Alfonso Reyes (whom Gabriela regarded as a master and whom she met for the first time in 1924 when she was in Paris with Palma Guillén), Ventura García Calderón and his brother Francisco García Calderón, Gonzalo Zaldumbide, Eduardo Santos (who was to become President of the Republic of Colombia in 1938), Mariano Brull, Teresa de la Parra, Víctor Andrés

Belaúnde, Alberto Zerega-Fombona, and Ruy Ribeiro Couto.

In the autumn of 1928, Gabriela again visited Spain to attend the International Conference of University Women at Madrid, as delegate from Chile and Ecuador. She stayed at the Home for Young Ladies, directed by her friend María de Maeztu. Margot Arce de Vázquez who met her at that time thus described her: ". . . She walked toward us with a remotedness, bearing upon her shoulders the weariness of centuries. A woolen cape fell below her knees and emphasized her gentle sway like that of a river; God was the constant thought, the daily preoccupation of Gabriela Mistral: God, love, and Latin America." [27]

In her conversations she revealed her love and concern for America, her nostalgia for the people and the landscape of the American countries. Although she lived away from her continent, she remained closely related to all aspects of American life through her daily reading and her contact with her Latin American friends. On September 26, 1928, she was appointed by the Council of the League of Nations to an important position in the Administrative Council of the Educative Institute of Cinematography, established in Rome. The Council had been created through a subsidy from the Italian Government. While in Italy, Gabriela prepared the necessary material for an Italian version of *Sleeping Beauty* by Charles Perrault.[28] In October, 1928, she wrote from Avignon to the Minister of Colombia about the Colombian volumes of the Collection; • in November, she was asked by the International Institute of Intellectual Cooperation to prepare a list of the principal periodicals of South America; in December, she reported to the Institute about the literary and scientific societies of Chile; and on February 14, 1929, she sent data on the Chilean Biological Institute. During 1928, she played an important part in the incorporation of Spain into the Institute in the person of Eugenio d'Ors whom she had recommended warmly as a great writer and journalist. In a letter of March 12, 1928, to the Director of the Institute, she wrote about the appointment of Eugenio d'Ors: ". . . Besides the entering of Spain into the Institute, this appointment offers the advantage of having a first-rate delegate: a great writer, journalist, member of the Academy and a man with a European spirit . . . On my return to Paris, next summer, I intend to take steps to have another Latin American country enter the Institute. I would like to be of some positive use in the affairs of Latin America."[29]

In 1928, Gabriela went to live in the small city of Bédarrides, Vaucluse, between Orange and Avignon, in Provence. The house was called Villa Saint-Louis and on the gate of the garden were the words "Property of the League of Nations." (She only traveled to attend meetings in Paris, Geneva, or Rome.) The garden was large and verdant and in it Gabriela spent some of her time, watering the plants early in the morning and giving them loving care. She lived in Bédarrides with her four-year-old nephew Juan Miguel Godoy, whom she affectionately called Yin-Yin, and to whom she gave her maternal love, and with Pradera Urquieta, a young Chilean woman who kept house for her. Among the many young writers who benefited from her spiritual guidance were Andrés Iduarte and Jorge Carrera Andrade. Iduarte, who stayed at her home of Bédarrides from April 18 to August 8, 1929, compared her to St. Teresa because of her indefatigable fight for justice. Her conversation could be about earthly as well as spiritual matters, and if at times she appeared ethereal, her great concern for, and love of, humanity made it impossible for her ever to withdraw from life. She saw social Christianity as the salvation of mankind.

Iduarte and Carrera Andrade, who witnessed at first hand that period of Gabriela's life, recall how she went to church every Sunday, believed in the evil power of the devil, and because of her mysticism cast aside all worldly concerns. She believed in disciplining herself as well as those around her, and she impressed upon herself and her home as austere convent-like, religious atmosphere. Nevertheless, this aspect of her personality was counterbalanced by a great warmth and a keen sense of humor. She knew how to laugh, and her smile would illuminate and soften her face.

Gabriela was a purifier at heart and all those who came in contact with her were, willingly or not, drawn into a spiritual world. "In the humble decor of the garden, Gabriela Mistral with her overpowering presence, her hair pulled back and her majestic and noble bearing, found herself in a befitting atmosphere. . . . A holy gardener who waged a pure war against disorder, dryness, and death, in defense of youth, hope, and life."[30] She considered this world an imposed terrestrial exile, but at the same time looked at the earth with wonder, marveling at all the hidden beauties to be discovered. She imposed upon herself a constant vagabondage or, sometimes, it was forced upon her. She felt that it was her duty not to remain in a country, but to belong to all. Gabriela would have liked to be endowed with the imaginative eyes of a five-year-old who experiences a close contact with nature. She often dreamed of reincarnation so that she could be born again as a child, each time in a different country, and never know the world as a satiated adult, or an indifferent outsider:

"It is only as a child that I would consent to come back to this world. To live in the same body for forty years, to eat the fruits of the same climate for half a lifetime holds no attraction for me. I find no incentive in going out and seeing the world or in paying formal calls on foreign landscapes when my poor senile eyes can only see the rock and no longer the mermaid who rests upon it; when my voice can only speak the word 'forest' and I can no longer see the elves of light that pierce the foliage from all sides."[31]

She did not want merely to pass like a visitor through a country, but she felt the need of absorbing each one, in order to take root in it. She continuously felt the need to move further in search of perfection, taking with her the memories of all the places she had known: "Houses do not tie me down. A month after I had bought my home in Santiago, I left for Mexico; a year after the one in La Serena I flew to Europe. An evil genie makes fun of me each time that I select a place to live in peacefully."[32]

The year 1929 was a crucial one in the evolution of her faith, for on July 7, her beloved mother died in La Serena at the age of 84. Jorge Carrera Andrade and César Arroyo broke the news to her. They had received a cablegram from Chile at the Consulate of Ecuador where Gabriela often received her mail. She had had a presentiment of her mother's death and, as she was told the news, there arose from her lips a moving prayer created spontaneously under her deep sorrow. Carrera Andrade, who was present, recalled to me in a personal interview the words created by her grief as she came face to face with the immense and irrevocable fact of death. Although not himself religious, he told me that he was deeply stirred by this spiritual outpouring. Gab-

riela was attached to her mother to whom she looked up as a
sacred being. At the time of her mother's death she confided in
a Chilean friend, the diplomat and poet Humberto Díaz Casa-
nueva, and said: "You must know that my saintly mother passed
away, that beautiful little old lady who was my only tie with
Chile. My spirits have fallen into ashes."[33] To another friend,
Ida Corbat, she wrote: "My mother was for me a presence that
sustained me. I almost never lived with her because of her attachment to La Serena; but she was my reason for being alive.
Now I have called my sister; she is all that I have and she is
very ill."[34] In a letter to Benjamín Carrión she spoke of the irremediable grief, of the severing from her of the only being who
was hers in this world.[35] In an explanatory note to her poem
"Muerte de mi madre" (Death of my Mother), published in
Tala (Felling of Trees), she said: "I have returned to this life
in a very compact darkness to repeat, as in the last words of
Desolación, the praise of happiness. The terrifying trip ends in
the hope found in the wild litanies and tells of its final moments
to those who care for my soul and know little of me since I
wander through life."[36]

Because of her firm belief in eternal life, Gabriela did not
rebel against her mother's death as she would have done in her
youth. With her grief came the certainty of a future life. There
is reason to believe that this change occurred in her after the
reading of the work of Henri Bergson *Les deux sources de la religion et de la morale* (The Two Sources of Religion and of
Morality).[37] The authorities of the city of La Serena took part
in her mother's funeral. After the memorial service in the church
of San Francisco, the casket was taken to the cemetery. The
Public High School for Boys and the Public High School for
Girls as well as delegations from all the primary schools and
the Normal School and School of Mines were there.

The presence of her mother was never to leave Gabriela, and
she dedicated to her some of her most beautiful poems included
in the section "Muerte de mi madre" of her book *Tala,* published in 1938:

> *Oh mother, in my dreams*
> *I walk through tortuous landscapes.*
> *I climb a dark mountain*
> *beyond which there always is outlined another,*

where undefined you stand,
but there is still another mount to overcome
to make my way
to the mountain of my rejoicing with you. [38]

In *Lagar* (Wine Press), 1954, the last book published in her lifetime, she continued to sing of her love to the "most faithful and most loved being":

My mother was very tiny
like mint or herbs
she hardly cast a shadow
upon things, hardly,
and the earth loved her
because of her being so light
and because she smiled at it
when happy and when sad.

Children were fond of her,
so were the old, so was the grass,
so was the light that looks for gracefulness,
loves it, and courts it. [39]

During Gabriela's last years, as probably throughout her life, the picture of her mother stood by her side in her bedroom and it accompanied her to the hospital where she was to spend her last days.

In spite of her mourning, Gabriela continued her active work at the Institute of Intellectual Cooperation, and she also represented Chile in Madrid at the International Conference of University Women. [40]

While in Bédarrides, Gabriela guided her friends in their reading of Latin American writers and talked to them about the destiny of America. She was very concerned about the fate of her Mexican Friend José Vasconcelos and wanted to form a group of "Friends of Vasconcelos" to help him during his political exile. She was obsessed by the struggle of the races and would speak often of her Basque and Indian origins. New books from all over Latin America reached her and it was said by the Ecuadoran poet Jorge Carrera Andrade that, according to their moral and literary value, they would either find an honored place in her home or a burial in the empty well situated in the garden: "There was below Gabriela's bedroom window a dried up well which had become the common burial grounds of books, a small dusty hell where those of little value were submitted to torture by an army of ants, water beetles, and other summer imps. This was the well of books!"[41]

Some of the writers she then admired were Alberti, Barbusse, Bernanos, Díez Canedo, Duhamel, Gide, Jammes, Antonio Machado, Mallarmé, Martí, Maurois, Anna de Noailles, Quevedo, Alfonso Reyes, Romain Rolland, St. Francis of Assisi, Tagore, Tolstoy, Unamuno, and Whitman.[42] She spoke warmly of Mariano Azuela, Rufino Blanco Fombona, Pedro Henríquez Ureña, Martín Luis Guzmán, José Vasconcelos, and in Ventura García Calderón she saw an interpreter of the American landscape.

Gabriela had a great love for books and she dreamed of having one day her own printing press in her home. She had observed the book business and saw that to the American public the format of books was important. She did not believe in the publication of skimpy books, for to her this signified a lack of generosity on the part of the author as well as a lack of respect for books. In her letters to Benjamín Carrión she advised him on publication matters and her comments reflected her almost religious attitude toward books. In 1930, she thought of having Marcel Vuillermoz publish a collection of some of her articles under the titles *Motivos franciscanos (Franciscan Motives), Estampas (Vignettes),* and *Elogios de las materias (Eulogy of the Elements),* and also a selection of articles she had written during her various trips. These plans did not come to fruition and the articles remained scattered in various newspapers and magazines: ". . . For all this I need time to select material and I will not be able to do it before next year. Among these articles there are some about my trips and various other things that are written with care."[43]

Thus, during that fertile period of her life she wrote, in addition to her poetry, beautiful pieces in prose. According to Luis Alberto Sánchez and Jorge Carrera Andrade, they are the best prose of Latin America, for she restored this genre of writing and ennobled it. She brought back to poetry and prose a new, personal approach, a message which she called *recado,* and which contained the striking vital qualities of the spoken language. The *recado* in prose was an essay written with the familiar flavor of her epistolary prose and conversation, and also the beauty of her poems in prose. The *recado* in poetic form possessed the same directness and warmth, with an effective and persuasive vitality. Her own explanation of this genre is very revealing: "The *recado* is an expression of that which is most authentic in me, it is the tone most often used by me and that reflects the rural world in which I lived and in which I am going to die."[44]

Out of her love for the pure and the primitive, she was attracted by medieval society and preached manual work as a means of finding a better world. She wrote much on artisans and their crafts and on those who loved their work: Bernard Palissy, one of the creators of French ceramics in the sixteenth century, Frédéric Mistral, who besides being a writer was one of the founders of the Museum of Arles, Séverine, the woman apostle of justice, and many others. Gabriela said on one occasion: "I travel looking for crafts. And in Italy I will continue searching for them. It is a lovely form of art."[45] She was later to exclaim in an interview in Spain: "I am a lover of craftsmanship and I feel a genuine affection for popular art, in spite of the fact that it is on its decline."[46] In her article "Los perfumes de Grasse" (Perfumes from Grasse) she made the picking of flowers appear as a most beautiful métier for women, as she poetically described the violets, mimosas, roses, acacias, and revealed her love for nature as well as her deep knowledge of it. She identified herself with the women working in the fields and was reminded of the atmosphere of the American earth: "If it were not for sciatica that has taken hold of me now that I am in my forties, I would gladly have worked with those agile performers in the fields: to behold the form of a shrub, like that of a baby, and find myself within the radiance of its scent as well as that of the whole planted field. During each moment of respite, instead of taking part in the spicy comments of the women, I would have gazed upon one slope, then another, and that which is beyond and stretches down to the water below."[47] She wrote lives of St. Francis of Assisi, St. Theresa of Lisieux, Jean Marie Vianney, Curé of Ars, and other saints. Gabriela also wrote many poetic chronicles as a consequence of her travels in various countries. In 1930, she lived in many of the cities of Italy and called Florence "The prettiest city in the world."[48] She wrote about the hills that surround the city of Florence and compared them to young girls encircling the city with their arms. She also wrote about the hills that surround Sestri Levante and compared them to dancers. She enjoyed the towns on the Riviera and she saw in the Mediterranean a jovial sea, with a mother-like quality. Italy was perhaps one of the countries to which she remained most attached, for she felt a close bond between its people and those of Latin America.

At the end of 1930, Gabriela made her second visit to the United States. There she taught at Barnard College, Columbia University, New York, where again she met Federico de Onís, at Vassar, Poughkeepsie, New York, and at Middlebury College, Vermont, where she gave a series of lectures on Chilean literature and Latin American literature in general. The pension that she received from Chile had been suspended (against President Ibáñez's wishes), and she had to live chiefly on what she earned from her articles and her teaching. She wrote for *El Tiempo* of Bogotá, *La Nación* of Buenos Aires, *El Universal* of Mexico, *El Repertorio Americano* of San José, Costa Rica, *El Mercurio* of Santiago, Chile, *ABC* of Madrid, *Nueva Democracia* of New York, and many other newspapers and magazines.

It was while she was in New York that the first book of the Ibero-American Collection came out: *Historiens chiliens* (Chilean Historians), in a French translation by Georges Pillement and with an introduction by Carlos Pereyra. At the International Institute of Intellectual Cooperation she was replaced by her friend Palma Guillén, as she had been before by Gonzalo Zaldumbide, Mariano Brull, Manuel Ugarte, and Eugenio d'Ors. From Santiago, Chile, an article on the League of Nations and Latin America, written by Francisco Walker Linares, revealed the importance of Gabriela's role in the Ibero-American Collection: ". . . The initiative for the Collection is due in great part to Gabriela Mistral."[49] Dominique Braga wrote to her in June, 1931, thanking her for her great participation in the Collection: "I always welcome your letters that bear witness to the interest you manifest for this Collection that is so indebted to you."[50]

Gabriela was asked in 1931 to teach a course at the University of Puerto Rico where she also gave several lectures. While in Puerto Rico she took the initiative in requesting a subsidy for the publication of a volume of the works of Eugenio María Hostos. During her stay she was deeply moved by the beauty of the

Puerto Rican landscape and her love of it never left her, as can be seen in her poetry and prose. She called Puerto Rico "her" island, praised every element within it, and rejoiced at the closeness with the sea which for her embodied the qualities of a father and a mother.

"The sea is everywhere. A few steps and you leave it behind; a few steps and you find it again. This is the magic of Puerto Rico and of all islands. In other lands the sea is an ornament for the eye and a taste of salt on the lips. On an island the taste of salt is constantly in your mouth like a grain of salt that clings to the corners of your lips. If the sea is like a father because of its appearance, it is also like a mother because of its soft taste."[51]

After this visit to the Antilles, she traveled in the Central American countries where she was greeted warmly. Everywhere she went, she spoke of the work of the International Institute of Intellectual Cooperation and of the Ibero-American Collection. After her meeting with the President of Panama she expressed the desire that a volume on the folklore of Panama be included in the Collection. The area of folklore was very important to Gabriela for it had been part of her life since childhood. With Alfonso Reyes she wanted to collect the folklore of all Latin America. She wrote in a letter: ". . . I think it will be necessary to enlarge greatly these volumes of American folklore, and that it would be very interesting, even, to have a volume representing every country. This is the only original literature we have. . . ."[52] She had proposed that the second Chilean volume consist of the country's folklore and she had hoped for a prologue by Ramón Menéndez Pidal, the great Spanish specialist in medieval literature and founder of the Center of Historic Studies in Madrid. Gabriela had also planned to visit Colombia in October of that year and to raise the necessary funds for the great romantic novel *María* by Jorge Isaacs which had been translated into French by Mathilde Pomès for the Collection, but she was unable to do so on account of her health. Once more Dominique Braga wrote of her contribution to the Collection: "I was happy to receive the long letter of Miss Mistral and to see how deep an interest she manifests for the Collection."[53] In November she took a trip to Germany with her friend Palma Guillén, and in December they arrived in Italy and stayed in Santa Margherita.

The year 1932 marked a new phase in the life of Gabriela Mistral as she entered the diplomatic service as Consul of Chile. She was appointed consul in Naples, but could not exercise her functions because of the fascist régime: ". . . I came to Naples appointed as Consul for my country. I had given myself three months to learn this new work . . . and it so happens that Mr. Mussolini decided not to accept women for such positions. Therefore, and in spite of the courteous exchange of letters between the two ministries, I have felt it my duty to resign."[54] In March, 1932, after she attended the meeting of the Publication Committee in Paris, she was again in Bédarrides where she stayed a few months; in June she was in Avignon, and in December she was in Lavagne, Province of Genoa. In January, 1933, she went to Barcelona and in March she again went to Puerto Rico where she stayed until June. She gave a series of lectures at the University of Puerto Rico at Río Piedras and set up a Committee for raising funds necessary for the publication of a volume of Hostos' work. Braga wrote to her: ". . . Once again you have given to the Latin American Collection, which owes its creation to you, another proof of your interest which has shown through in such an effective manner."[55]

Shortly after she left Puerto Rico for Spain in July, 1933, the Rector of the university, Carlos Chardon, wrote of her to Braga: " . . . The famous Chilean writer Gabriela Mistral embarked a few days ago for Madrid but the seeds of her undertakings have blossomed in the form of the creation of a Committee charged with the raising of funds for the future publication of Hostos in translation."[56] In Spain she replaced Víctor Domingo Silva as honorary consul in Madrid, a position that carried no stipend. She lived mainly on newspaper articles published in Spain and Latin America and on her savings put aside from her teachings in the United States and Puerto Rico. Among some of her Spanish friends were Miguel de Unamuno, Ramiro and María de Maeztu, Blanca de los Ríos, Enrique and Teresa Díez Canedo, Salvador de Madariaga, Carmen Conde and her husband Antonio Oliver Belmás, Angel Valbuena Prat, Concha Espina, María Martínez Sierra, and Victoria Kent.

Senhora Ribeiro Couto, the wife of the late Brazilian poet and diplomat Ruy Ribeiro Couto, recounted to me a trip to Spain that her husband had taken in the same car with Gabriela Mistral and Miguel de Unamuno. They spoke, she said, in an inspiring and passionate way of the vital topics that mattered to them: Spain, Latin America and, of course, the fate of the Indian.

Both Gabriela and Don Miguel were deeply religious and they both had tormented and searching souls. They were bound by their same Basque origin, a similar faculty for disclosing the essential characteristics of their people, and for leading them into a spiritual awakening. Both writers were exponents of their nations and wanted each person to become conscious of his own identity. Unamuno once pointed out: "I have tried to give them an understanding of what they are";[57] and Gabriela, turning to her own continent, wrote: "We must cultivate a type of patriotism which will be none other than our capacity to depict with filial love our mountain range, our rivers, the miraculous land upon which we walk."[58] I recall that one day in 1956, when I was spending the afternoon with her, Gabriela showed me a picture of Unamuno and asked me to pray for the soul of her Spanish friend who had died in 1936. She spoke of him as if twenty years had not elapsed, for to her the passage of time did not matter. She often spoke of her past as if it were part of the present just as she spoke of the countries she had known as if they were part of one country.

Gabriela remained consul in Madrid until 1935 and throughout those years her consulate was open to all. Her Mexican friend Palma Guillén, lived with her in Spain during her vacations and spent between three to six months with her when Gabriela needed her. For example, Palma remained in Spain six months with Gabriela between 1934 and the beginning of 1935 until she herself was appointed Minister plenipotentiary of Mexico in the Republic of Colombia. During her residence in Spain, Gabriela visited Barcelona, Málaga, and other parts of the country. In Málaga, she gave a lecture on Chile called "Breve descripción de Chile" *(A Brief Description of Chile),* published in 1934 in Santiago by the Press of the University of Chile. A series of poems were also published that year under the title "Nubes blancas" *(White Clouds).* An article that appeared at the time said that to speak of Gabriela Mistral in Spain was like mentioning the Countess of Pardo Bazán, for she was well known as a writer and admired for her contributions to the Spanish press and her generosity to all.[59] Dr. Oliver Belmás, in a letter to me, related how Gabriela would share her table and her library with him and his wife Carmen Conde: ". . . Both Carmen and I would sit at her table, read in her study and one night she even gave up her bed so that we could stay over."[60] Andrés Iduarte and many others found the same warm reception. Pedro Juan Labarthe wrote that all Puerto Ricans who arrived in Madrid came directly to the consulate of Chile where they would find a home and a friend.[61]

Gabriela would invite her friends or welcome persons she did not know but who needed her help, and with them she would talk for hours after they had eaten a frugal dinner together. Her conversation, which consisted of dissertations on various subjects, anecdotes, Chilean tales and folklore, imparted, as Victoria Kent rightly said, "a creative and tangible luminosity which can never be reproduced."[62] If all her conversations could have been recorded, they would form a beautiful work of art, embodying the aesthetic as well as the earthy in a way which was essentially hers. Víctor Andrew Belaúnde, while President of the General Assembly of the United Nations, imparted to me the value of her conversations and compared them to a perfume. The Argentine writer and great friend of Gabriela, Victoria Ocampo, who had first met her in Madrid in 1930, spoke to me with fondness of Gabriela's characteristic manner of speech, and of her abrupt frankness. At their first meeting, Gabriela had jokingly reproached her for having been born in Buenos Aires, the least Latin American city of the Continent, for being a Francophile, and for not having been a close friend of the Argentine poet Alfonsina Storni. Gabriela's conversations became beautiful monologues that enthralled and mystified everyone who came within her circle. Victoria Ocampo wrote of her: "To hear her speak was like a miracle, through her voice we listened to America. Words have a new flavor when they are selected and pronounced by her."[63]

It was while consul in Madrid that Gabriela made the discovery that the language which had been spoken by her mother and by herself, tinted with a certain archaic element, was the same as that of the Spanish men of letters. Gabriela would often say with a gentle and yet mischievous smile: "I speak a borrowed language"[64] and in the same manner would refer to Spain as her "mother country." However, her archaic expressions, similar to those found in the classical period of Spain, was not a literary pose; it was something natural in her which she had inherited from the language spoken in her Valley of Elqui; a language preserved and kept alive in the towns hemmed in by the Andes Mountains since the Spanish Conquest of Latin America. Gabriela proved more than once her spiritual and cultural attachment to Spain. She wanted children to learn their own language carefully and she looked upon it with a religious reverence. In an article about the language of José Martí, she mentioned that the Cuban hero who fought against Spain for the independence of his country was at the same time united to Spain by his concern for Spanish, their common language: "He kept his loyalty to Spain, the true loyalty we owe this country—that of the language."[65]

Her attitude toward Spain was twofold. She remembered the evils of the Spanish conquest and the maltreatment of the Indians by the Spanish *encomenderos;*[66] nevertheless, she felt close to the Spanish people and to their needs and she could not shut her eyes to the problems of Spain during the Civil War. She did not love Spain as a foreigner, but as a daughter who knew its virtues and its flaws. She looked at Spain with the same realistic and loving attitude that she had for her own continent in her endeavor to raise the standard of living of the people. She knew by heart every region of Spain, but without doubt she felt closest to the Basque people to whom she was related by blood.

Gabriela was a daughter who could not forget the kindred spirit that drew her to the Spanish mystics. Already in 1925 during her first visit to Spain she had written a moving article on St. Teresa of Avila, as she passed through Castile. In her imagination it was the saint who had made her understand that part of Spain, who had guided her with love, and had conversed with her about the differences and similarities of Spain and Latin America: "She tells me: Won't you let me show you Castile, my region, so that you may come to understand it? . . . I can be your guide up to the border with Portugal with no need of asking questions. Now they make maps for those who travel. I scanned my Castile walking; I carry a living map on the sole of my feet, daughter. I never tire of laying foundations. You, woman of Chile, without having set up foundations, are weary."[67] The "traveling nun" had founded seventeen convents for women and fifteen for men with the help of St. John of the Cross, in the face of human opposition. Victoria Kent wrote of Gabriela's attitude toward Spain:

". . . She loved Spain in all its regions, that is to say, in all its traits . . . and her knowledge of and devotion to the Spanish classics were superior to those of many Spaniards who take themselves for ardent scholars. Her powerful Castilian prose has its roots in Gracián and St. Teresa, her poetry has a personal touch, but through it shines her intimacy with Spanish mystics."[68] To one of her translators, Mathilde Pomès, Gabriela appeared to have an eternal Spanish moral depth. She possessed the strength of the spirit of Queen Isabella of Spain and St. Teresa. She also possessed the same moral integrity as Unamuno and spiritually resembled Antonio Machado and García Lorca. We can add that her style of writing has much of the strength and warmth of St. Teresa and St. John of the Cross. In their works, as in hers, there is simplicity and spontaneity. Gabriela introduced vernacular expressions to give verve and vitality to the language and, like them, used concrete and abstract terms to describe the invisible world in her mystic flight toward the unattainable. Her neologism consists of bringing back archaic words, either of learned or popular origin, of introducing indigenous terms, or of coining new words. Both St. Teresa and Gabriela liked to improvise when they did not find words that suited their needs, both could have been called "restless travelers" in their spiritual pursuit, an expression used by Father Jerónimo Gracián when describing the Spanish saint.

Gabriela contributed to Spanish newspapers, especially *ABC* and *El Sol* of Madrid, and her articles expressing her admiration and respect for many Spanish writers, as well as her comprehension of the Spanish landscape, were published throughout Latin America.

Some of her criticisms of Spain which came out of her concern for the Spanish people were misconstrued and her affection was misunderstood. A letter she had written to a friend in which she spoke of Spain in a violent and passionate tone was made public. Following this incident, Gabriela said that in Chile forty-three articles were written against her and only six in her favor. Gabriela reacted against this false accusation and undertook her own defense in an article in which she wrote: "I admit willingly that my letter had a rather violent tone; those who have kept company with the Hebrew prophets will know that filial disappointment and respect can be expressed with outright violence."[69] In an interview in the same year, 1938, she said: "From Portugal, I have felt as a personal hurt the tragedy of Spain. I did not sleep many times thinking about the suffering of its people. I overheard the battering noise of the bombardment. I imagined the terror of the defenseless inhabitants and it grieved me."[70] Her deep concern for the fate of Spain is perhaps best expressed by her act of generosity and love when in 1938 she turned over the proceeds of her book *Tala* for the benefit of the children who had been left homeless by the Spanish Civil War.

In August, 1935, a group of European writers, including Miguel de Unamuno, Guglielmo Ferrero, Romain Rolland, Georges Duhamel, and Maurice Maeterlinck, addressed a petition to the President of Chile, Arturo Alessandri Palma, asking that Gabriela be given a paid consulate that would assure her economic security. In this effort they were supported by a large group of Chilean writers and friends of Gabriela's. A bill was drafted and, with the support of the President and of Gustavo Rossi, Minister of Finance, it became a special law, passed by the legislature and signed by the President on September 17, 1935. It created for Gabriela Mistral the post of consul *per vita* that would allow her to live in whatever country she chose.[71] Gabriela never used this office as a sinecure and always took an active part in the activities of her consulate. She helped Chileans abroad and other Latin Americans, wrote reports, and kept in touch with the Latin American continent. In a letter to Arturo Alessandri, she revealed her deep gratitude:

"There is no possible way for me, a person for whom the past continues to live on in the present, to forget President Alessandri. If our chief executive had not been a man of letters, the message sent in my behalf by European writers would have remained unanswered, thrown away in some waste paper basket. But you read it, you gave it some consideration and you answered it with the nobility of character with which God endowed you and which life was not able to dent nor destroy. You are in the daily prayers of your *paisana* (fellow Chilean) who is not an ungrateful person."[72]

In October, 1935, Gabriela was transferred to Lisbon as second class consul. Here she began to appreciate the rich Portuguese literature and learn to love its soft and suave language. Often she would speak to me of the Portuguese idiom and praise it. Once more her consulate became the refuge of all those who needed a helping hand. Adelaida Portillo, the first wife of Andrés Segovia, thus described to me how she was welcomed into the warm circle of Gabriela Mistral:

"I arrived in Lisbon completely depressed, I knew that Gabriela Mistral was serving as consul there and without being acquainted with her, I came to her door. She took me in like a harbor that gives refuge and her magical circle closed in on me from that moment. It is to her that I owe having regained my equilibrium for she had the exceptional gift of placing herself and placing others on a spiritual sphere outside of the depressing zone of reality. I remember her words: 'One must sublimate one's life. It is necessary to be on the alert, to be faithful and joyful in order to fill a well with rejoycing in anticipation of eternity.' Gabriela was as captivating as a beam of light and as warm as a hearth. For me, to speak of Gabriela is like speaking of the delta of a river."[73]

On November 25, 1936, Gabriela came to Paris to attend a meeting of the Publication Committee of the Collection and she proposed to form a subcommittee, presided over by her friend Professor Paul Rivet, to collect the necessary materials for the publication of the volume on Chilean folklore.

In February, 1937, Gabriela received in Lisbon a letter from Dominique Braga announcing that she had been named a member of the Committee on Letters and Arts and that she was to take part in the Literary Talk to be held in Paris: "You must have received the official invitation which was sent from Switzerland. I am writing this note to your home to confirm the invitation as a member of the Committee on Letters and Arts to the Talk to be held in July."[74] Gabriela had just come back from a long trip through France, Germany, and Denmark. She spent some time in Copenhagen with her friend Palma Guillén who was Minister Plenipotentiary to Denmark (1937-1938).[75]

The Literary Talk of the Committee on Letters and Arts in which she took part was held in Paris, July 20-23, 1937, with Paul Valéry presiding. Some of the writers invited to the conference were: Georges Duhamel, Paul Hazard, Jules Romains, Miguel Osorio de Almeida, Francisco Garcia Calderón, and André Rousseaux. The theme discussed was: "The Future Destiny of Letters." During the conference, Gabriela spoke of the economic situation of the American writer and of the difficult struggle of the poet. Here is a section of her speech in defense of the poet in which she shows her desire to help him:

"I think that it is necessary to take into consideration the very special position of poets.

"The poet is a human being separated from the rest of mankind. He is the most helpless of creatures in his struggle for life. It is very seldom that poets are capable of doing something else to earn their living, and besides, I believe that poets are right in not wanting to do anything else. But what can we do for them? Could we perhaps create an international prize for poetry? No one thinks about poetry. Even among our people who are very sensitive and fond of poetry, when we contemplate the distribution of prizes, we always think of the novel and the theater, but never think of poetry. I would be very happy to work with Latin American governments to make them interested in this matter. Indeed, poetry is held in great esteem by everyone, but it is also easily forsaken by all. This is a sad reality. One values poets and at the same time looks down on them; we carry this position so far that we find it odd to protect them, for down deep in ourselves we believe that poetry, just as the sun or the rain, should be some kind of gratuitous and God-sent gift."[76]

During the Paris conference, Massimo Pilotti said of Gabriela Mistral: "Gabriela Mistral is a poet dear to us. She reminds me of an Italian poet, perhaps the greatest since Petrarque. (This phrase is not mine, it is that of another Italian poet: d'Annunzio). This great poet, who died before the war, in 1912, and whose name is Giovanni Pascoli."[77] Henri Bonnet, Director of the Institute from 1931 to 1939 and later Ambassador of France to various countries, said to me on one occasion: "Gabriela Mistral was part of the Committee on Letters and Arts which was presided over by Paul Valéry. She devoted her whole being to the task of preserving peace."

At the end of August, 1937, Gabriela left for Brazil, a trip she had planned since 1936. In São Paulo, she was made an honorary member of the "Brazilian Pan American Society" for her high merits as a priestess of American brotherhood.[78] In Rio de Janeiro, she read to the children of the Institute of Education her poem "Cuenta mundo" ("Tales of the World"). She recited it again to the children of the school Luis Delfino, after planting a Brazilian tree in the courtyard of the school.[79]

From Brazil she went to Argentina where she was greatly admired for the clarity of her thoughts and her simplicity. It was written of her: "If it could be said of a person that he has gone through the labyrinth of knowledge and grasped its meaning, it is certainly of this well-known Latin-American woman who speaks great truths with the simplicity of one who knows in depth the roots of life."[80] She, in turn, felt a close bond with Argentine women: "As I listen to my sisters I am reminded of a quality of light found in our mountains, a soft and sharp light. I have signed with pleasure and pride the book of the League of Argentine women because I have received from this group the warmth so typical of our generous America."[81] When she learned of the death of Leopoldo Lugones, the noted Argentine writer, she expressed her spiritual debt to him and her great sorrow: "I was in Uruguay when Lugones died. I had never known him personally, and nevertheless I valued him and loved him through his work. The news was terrible for me. Lugones had an exceptional rich and warm personality. He loved children as I do. How sweetly he wrote stories for them. I am indebted to him."[82] It was also through Lugones that she came to know more deeply the work of Domingo Faustino Sarmiento, the great educator and writer and President of Argentina from 1868 to 1874.

In Buenos Aires, in a recital sponsored by the magazine *Sur* owned by Victoria Ocampo, Gabriela spoke of her poetry, something she seldom did, explaining some of her poems and then read them to the audience. She also spoke on other occasions of the Chilean poet Pablo Neruda and said of him:

"Before him, the poetry of my country vegetated. There were prose writers, but no poets. . . . Sorrow and sadness vibrate in his verse, because we, the people of Chile, are sad people.

"I met him when he was a young boy in that southern town where he was born. Neruda grew up gazing at a landscape that receives throughout the year the bitterness of rain. As a result, a serene sadness remained at the core of all his poems."[83]

She sent Dominique Braga a preface she had undertaken to write for the volume of *Folklore Chilien* (Chilean Folklore), which was translated by Georgette and Jacques Soustelle, and published in July, 1938, by the International Institute of Intellectual Co-operation. Gabriela described realistically the customs of the Araucanian Indians and expressed her deep understanding of them. The book meant more to her than a collection of colorful Chilean folklore. It meant that European writers would be able to understand through this selection of folklore the actions and the thoughts of the Chilean Indian, his love of the mountain and of the sea:

"In the tale of Tren-Tren . . . the Indian does not forsake his vision of the mountains, for no man from Chile can have a thought in which the Cordillera is not reflected; but it is the sea that dominates; the Indian has created his story face to face with the ocean, wrongly named Pacific, a sea truly in turmoil, beaten by the southern winds and blended with the sky into an angry and mysterious mass, which is appropriate for fables and tales of passion." [84]

"We poets have always known that the poetic life, the poetic method, the poetic style of man and life, whether they be those of an Arab, Hindu, Mexican or Quechua, are deep and serious matters; not just the ornamentation on a canister or on a multi-colored rug." [85]

Dominique Braga wrote to Jacques Soustelle of that preface: "Miss Mistral has a distinctive warmth which shows the interest that she bears for her beloved Indians." [86]

While in Buenos Aires, Gabriela was invited by Victoria Ocampo to spend a few weeks with her in her home in Mar del Plata. (In 1924 another well-known guest, Rabindranath Tagore, had stayed there.) As was her custom, Gabriela would sit for hours after a frugal dinner, smoking cigarette after cigarette, talking on and on. She took great joy in children, and the child of the gardener was sweet company for her. She never spoke of her literary work, nor gave any precise details about her own life. Gabriela spent happy and restful days in the villa and stayed until April 7, her birthday as well as that of Victoria Ocampo. To commemorate this coincidence, Gabriela dedicated to Victoria the poem "Recado a Victoria Ocampo en la Argentina" (Message to Victoria Ocampo in Argentina), in which she praised her and her land, the beauty of the countryside, and poetically entrusted to her the safeguarding of the freedom of America:

*Thank you for the sweet dreams that your home
offered me,*

. . . .

*I say farewell and I leave you
as I found you, seated on the dune,
I entrust you with the lands of Latin America,
you who are so much like a ceiba tree, and like a
flamingo,
so completely Andean and so flowing,
a rushing waterfall,
lightning from the Pampa.* [87]

Gabriela Mistral's third book of poetry, *Tala* (Felling of Trees), appeared in 1938. Sixteen years had elapsed since the publication of *Desolación.* Her decision to publish this new book at that time instead of later was an act of generosity and love for the innocent Spanish children who had lost their homes and their parents during the Spanish Civil War. Victoria Ocampo financed *Tala,* which was issued by her own publishing house, Editorial Sur. The proceeds were sent by Gabriela as a gift to the Spanish children. In this gesture, motivated by her humanistic spirit, Gabriela revealed what she had always expressed in her poetry—her love for all children and for all those who suffered. It was also an expression of her solidarity toward Spain:

"One would have to be lacking in intelligence not to realize the suffering of Spain. But I want to make it clear that, in spite of the efforts of interested parties to narrow me down and encase me in a determined group, I have shown proof of my love for Spain with concrete actions and not just with words. I have helped as much as it was possible through the Institute of Intellectual Cooperation, the teachers who had fled their country and the poor Basque children who are scattered all over Europe. This was brought about by the publication of *Tala* in Buenos Aires to be sold in Latin America and in Barcelona for its European distribution. I admire a people which defends its territory and fights with such heroism." [88]

She explained the reason for publishing the book in these words: ". . . Now I offer *Tala* because I have nothing else to give the Spanish children scattered to the winds. Let them take this humble book from the hands of their Gabriela, who is partly

Basque. May *Tala* be cleansed of its essential imperfection through the act of helping, of being solely the instrument of my love toward the innocent blood of Spain that flows through the peninsula and through all of Europe.''[89] Gabriela had made the selection of poems for *Tala* while staying in Geneva with her friend Palma Guillén and it was to her that she dedicated it and through her paid her indebtedness to Mexico: "To Palma Guillén and, through her, to the loyalty of Mexican women."

The book consisted of many poems she had composed during her journeys in America and Europe. With the same warmth, they sang of all the countries she had known, the countries that through her love had become one, freed from all human boundaries. Her vision of the world was a poetic geography which embraced all the farthest landscapes, the memories both sweet and bitter: Chile, Mexico, the Antilles, Latin America as a whole, Provence, Italy, Spain, and later California, all the lands through which she had traveled and that she had loved. These all formed the background to her poem "País de la ausencia" (Land of Absence):

. . . .

It was born to me of things
that are not countries,
of homelands and homelands
that I had and I lost;
of the living things
that I have seen die,
of that which was mine
and left me. [90]

Concha Meléndez of Puerto Rico has rightly said that the actual geographical extension of countries did not coincide with the place Gabriela gave each one of them in her poetry.[91] Her imaginary map had its beginning in Chile where the small Valley of Elqui occupied for her most of the territory and was constantly a point of comparison. From there, in her outline of America, the Mexican Anáhuac appeared vaster than Brazil. In her love of America, she sang of the Indian corn of Anáhuac, the Panamanian drum, and the Caribbean sea. She looked up to the sun of the Incas and Mayas, the sun of the Andes, and to it she offered herself after a long absence:

> *Like the maguey, like the yucca,*
> *the Peruvian jug,*
> *thé calabash of Uruápan,*
> *the century old quena,*
> *I give myself to you, I yield,*
> *I open up, I bathe in you!*
> *Take me as you received them,*
> *with each pore and each kernel,*
> *and place me to live among them*
> *in ecstasy within your rapture.* [92]

But above all, she dedicated a majestic hymn to the Andes Mountain range, which symbolically unites in its chain all of Latin America:

> *May we invoke you in alleluias*
> *and in enraptured litanies:*
> *Eternal, suspended body,*
> *High up city, golden towers,*
> *paschal advent of your people,*
> *stretched Ark of the Covenant!* [93]

The flora and fauna of America were present in *Tala;* so also was the Indian who appeared everywhere as her brother, whether he was Mexican, Peruvian, or Chilean. *Tala* was in great part a hymn of praise to nature, to its simplest elements which Gabriela touched with a maternal and Franciscan love: bread, salt, water, fire, air. Her love of nature, of the earth, was so deep that each stone or flower she saw seemed to be caressed by her. Sometimes there almost seemed to be the same pagan element in her as in her "Indian ancestors" of which she spoke romantically. Francis de Miomandre, her translator and friend, rightly said: "It is no longer with the eyes of a master that we glance upon the elements of nature, but with the eyes of a brother. [94]

The critic Gastón Figueira thus explained *Tala:* ". . . It reflects the long experience of someone who has traveled the earth, enjoyed slowly the landscape and understood the typical colors of all of Latin America." [95] Sidonia Carmen Rosenbaum wrote: *"Tala,* published in 1938, is the vintage of sixteen years of intense and errant living . . . Its mastery, its sureness of style and precise choice of words reveal the mature artist who has gone through the bitter exercise of attaining that much prized 'difficult simplicity.' ''[96]

Tala was stripped of all selfish thoughts; it no longer expressed, as did *Desolación,* a passionate and fierce spirit that revealed the entire range of human love and pain. Even the section dedicated to her mother's death was serene, for Gabriela had reached a profound religious belief. As Palma Guillén said to me, Gabriela was above all religious; she had been interested in yoga, in Christian science, in all religions, and had returned to the simple faith of the first Christians.

Toward the end of 1937, Gabriela undertook a pilgrimage through Latin America, giving lectures in Brazil, Argentina, Uruguay, Chile, Peru, Cuba, and elsewhere, and ended her journey in the United States. In Uruguay she was invited to participate in the South American Summer Seminar organized in Montevideo. She also gave a lecture on Pablo Neruda, whom she greatly admired, and a record was made of her speech.[97] Together with the two great women poets Juana de Ibarbourou and Alfonsina Storni she took part in a public function held at the Institute of Secondary Education A. Vázquez Acevedo. Later, in an article about her friend and a well-known poet, Ester de Cáceres, she expressed her deep admiration for Uruguay, "the country of friendship"[98] as she called it.

In Chile, Gabriela was received with even greater honor than in 1925. There were popular and official receptions, and arches of triumph were erected in the streets. An enormous crowd gathered around her and listened to her unforgettable voice: "All her admirers fought over the privilege of kissing her hand, and she granted it wearily in a somewhat detached fashion, to her friends of many years as well as to the powerful or *nouveaux riches.*''[99] She had become the most acclaimed woman of Latin America although she shunned all honors. She pleaded with her friends to be received in silence, without celebrations: "Her heart sought peace and tranquility."[100] In one of the interviews in Chile, she revealed with a smile that she liked to go to the movies during the matinées to see cartoons, for she was happy to be among children: "If you could only know how I enjoy going to the matinées. I feel as if I were standing in the schoolyard surrounded by children at play. And I laugh and I laugh. For a moment I am truly happy."[101]

While in Chile, Gabriela spoke about her attitude toward writing. She confessed that she acquired the habit of getting up very early to work for two to three hours. She had learned this discipline in France, in her association with French writers who led a rigorous life and who did not believe in the sole power of inspiration, but whose method was one of constant revision. She said of them: "They have to write methodically. They do not wait, as we do, for inspiration or for the Muse to stand close by. To a certain point, this is a myth. The writer is a professional who masters his talent and who can write at any given time."[102] She could understand Lope de Vega, the Spanish dramatist of the Golden Age, author of more than four hundred plays, who believed that one should laugh at a poet who does not know how to erase. She never ceased being a craftsman striving for a finished product through divine grace and arduous work, and constantly aware of human frailty. Like her countryman Pablo Neruda, she held the belief that the poet is a worker who has a duty to perform; like Juan Ramón Jiménez, the 1956 Nobel Prize Winner from Spain, she understood that in perfecting one's work the poet comes closer to his Creator; like Frederico García Lorca, she believed that writing is partly a conscious act, partly the result of the magic power lent by a friendly spirit; like the mystics she could write under the fire of passion, and then when serenity had once again returned to her soul, she would go over her poetry with the scrutinizing eyes of an ascetic, casting away the superfluous. Gabriela wanted perfection in books so as not to disappoint the readers. To arrive at this perfection she sought simplicity, knowing that it is perhaps the most difficult achievement of true art. She was without doubt her own strongest and fiercest critic and in that sense was a classical writer. Paul Valéry once said: "Classical is the writer who carries a critic within himself and who binds him closely to his work."[103] In the Chilean Society of Writers she spoke of the necessity of creating a national prize for literature and she gave her views on the role of the writer. It is his responsibility to safeguard the Spanish language, to praise with it the beauty of the American continent, so as not to become oblivious of the native elements. Her own style, which shows great equilibrium, is a fusion of the learned and spoken language; it is both combative and merciful, strong and soft.

From Chile Gabriela went to Lima as a guest of the Peruvian

Government to give a few lectures. On July 8, 1938, Dominique Braga wrote to her about her journey: "I have followed your itinerary through Latin America since your departure from Lisbon by reading South American newspapers and some of your beautiful poetry published by *Sur.*"[104] In Cuba, she was hailed by the city of Havana as an apostle whose mission it was to unify the intellectual world of America. Dulce María Borrero de Luján praised her and among many things said: "The limpid, sharp thought, grieved or humble, soft and naked, like a biblical song, is characteristic of her; it is of a unique, inimitable, and sober architecture."[105] In a speech on that occasion, Gabriela said that she divided the world into three categories: countries of the Father, which were strong, countries of the Son, which were soft, and countries of the Holy Spirit, which were warm and fiery. Mexico and Cuba were part of the last named category, while Chile belonged to the first: "And I believe that the essence of Chile belongs to the Heavenly Father. We are strong and perhaps somewhat abrupt. The grace of the Holy Spirit seldom shines upon us."[106] She also spoke in another instance of the Cuban music which accompanied her in her European solitude: "Cuban music nourishes in me the native elements that I do not want to lose while in Europe, and which I watch over as the marrow of my bones."[107]

While in Cuba she spoke about José Martí, the Cuban poet who died on the battlefield in 1895 as he fought for his country's independence from Spain. She considered the influence of Martí on her work as the most important one exercised by a Latin American writer. She admired the virility and vitality of his style which was at the same time gentle and merciful. It was a composite of the best qualities of the Spanish Classical period and of the Latin America of his time; a complete language, endowed with popular and learned elements, rich and alive. But she also admired 'the spiritual quality of his whole being. The following lines embody his gentle philosophy of life which resembles her own:

When I was born, Nature said to me:
"Love!"
And my heart answered: "Give thanks!"
And since then I love the good and the bad,
faithfulness has become my religion
and I embrace all those who are kind to me.[108]

On October 30, 1938, Gabriela gave a lecture on José Martí, the man and the writer, which became the preface to his book *Versos sencillos* (Simple Verse), published in 1939. She revealed the profound tie that united her to him and to Cuba: "There is to be found my most successful dialogue with him; the beam of light transcends from his work to descend directly upon me."[109]

Later in the same year, Gabriela returned to Europe and was appointed consul in Nice. While she was there, a movement was started in Ecuador and Chile to make her the candidate of all of Latin America for the Nobel Prize. However, according to the critic Norberto Pinilla, the idea of the Nobel Prize for Gabriela Mistral had been initiated earlier by Virgilio Figueroa, author of *La divina Gabriela,* the first biography written about her and published in 1933. As Gabriela explained in an interview with United Press in Rio de Janeiro on November 15, 1945, her candidacy for the Nobel Prize had been proposed by a group of Ecuadoran writers, headed by her friend Adela Velasco, to the President of Chile, Pedro Aguirre Cerda. The President had asked Gabriel González Videla, Chilean Minister Plenipotentiary in France, to write to Gabriela Mistral about the Nobel Prize candidacy. After some delay, Gabriela wrote from Nice, where she then lived, that she believed that Rómulo Gallegos, Alfonso Reyes, Casiano Ricardo, and many others deserved more than she to be honored by Stockholm. Latin American literature, she wrote, was little known in Europe, and especially the works of poets, which were so difficult to translate. If they were to attract the attention of Stockholm, it was necessary that they be translated at least into French and English. Gabriela herself had had some of her poems translated into French by friends of hers who worked with her at the International Institute of Intellectual Cooperation. But she did not wish to use her position in the Institute as a means of furthering her candidacy:

"I have found out something about the action taken in Santiago to have the Nobel Prize granted me. It is an initiative started in Ecuador that also grew in Argentina.

"There are selections of poems of mine in French, translated by Miomandre, Pillement, Mathilde Pomès, Max Daireaux; but they have never been assembled in a book. The group of friends from Ecuador who have begun this movement on my behalf for the

Nobel Prize intend to do something about it. I personally do not want to have any part in this endeavor, although I feel very grateful for their generosity. I will *never* be a spokesman of my own literary renown, or of my own work."[110]

Her open letter to Pinilla, written in Niteroi, Brazil, in October, 1940, makes clear her attitude about the Nobel Prize: "I have never believed, nor will I believe now, in the effectiveness of my candidacy for the Nobel Prize, which originated in Ecuador and was welcomed by President Aguirre and then played upon, to such an extent, by other people and other Latin American nations."[111]

Up to that time, the only Spanish-speaking Nobel Prize laureates had been: José Echegaray (from Spain, 1904) for Literature, Santiago Ramón y Cajal (from Spain, 1906) for Medicine, Jacinto Benavente (from Spain, 1922) for Literature, Carlos Saavedra Lamas (from Argentina, 1936) for Peace. While the initiative for Gabriela's candidacy was being undertaken by her friends, she continued to work in Nice as consul. She had been designated in 1939 by President Aguirre Cerda as Extraordinary Envoy and Minister Plenipotentiary to the Central American governments, with her residence in San José, Costa Rica. She did not accept this high position, however, because of her excessive modesty.[112]

In 1939, some of her work, hitherto unpublished, appeared in Antonio Roco del Campo's anthology of Chilean national literature, *Panorama y color de Chile* (Panorama and Color of Chile), published by Ediciones Ercilla, Santiago, Chile. Among her prose writings were included "Chile," "Valle de Elqui" (Valley of Elqui), "Fresia," "El Caleuche" (The Caleuche), and "Algarrobos y espinos" (Carob Tree and Hawthorn), and among her poems were "Lago Llanquihue" (Lake Llanquihue), "Salto del Laja" (The Waterfall of Laja), and "Volcán Osorno" (The Osorno Volcano). These three poems had been written during her short stay in Chile in 1938 when she made a new and strong contact with the Chilean landscape. She had purified and strengthened her soul in the water of her native land:

> *Lake Llanquihue, Indian water,*
> *ancient radiance of the soil,*
> *water that is old and that is gentle,*
> *potion of centuries;*
> *water that is as lasting as the Indian*

and as cold and as fiery as he,
your chest is that of a mariner
whose tatoos are marked in green.

. . . .

I drink in your water what I have lost:
I drink the innocence of the Indian spirit;
I take in the heavens, I take in the earth,
I receive the homeland that you give back to me. [113]

Some of these works also appeared in the *Bulletin of the Pan American Union,* April, 1939.

While Gabriela was in Nice, plans were made for a volume of some of her poems and prose in French translations to be issued by Stock. Mathilde Pomès translated the poems and Francis de Miomandre translated the prose selections. Mathilde Pomès was to have delivered the manuscript to the publisher on July 1, 1940, but the project was interrupted by the outbreak of the Second World War.

In a conversation with me she recalled that she had completed the final translation of the poems during the bombardment of Paris. It was at her own request that Paul Valéry wrote a preface to introduce the Chilean poet to the European public. He knew her work only through the excellent translation of Mathilde Pomès and it was she who gave him the necessary information about Gabriela's life and work. In spite of a poetic temperament so different from that of the Chilean poet, his preface is of great interest because it reveals the reaction of a European who comes into contact with a great work outside his own culture, and a new element until then unknown to him:

"The first impression that this collection of her work made on me was like that of an encounter with an object or a human being totally different, but fundamentally real; surprising as when we discover that nature does create many more types and ways of existence than we could ever imagine.

". . . This woman sings of childhood as no one had ever done before. Mme Mistral expresses in a profoundly earnest and simple way the emotion of life in the presence of a newly created life. There is a physiological mysticism in her 'Song of the Blood,' where motherhood in its pure state exalts itself in lyrical and realistic terms: this mother sees her own blood in the newly born babe who sleeps with her taste of milk and blood . . ."[114]

Gabriela would never have asked Valéry to write a preface since she had always believed that an introduction to the work of a Spanish-speaking author should be written by someone who had a deep knowledge and understanding of Hispanic letters. She would rather have selected someone like Miomandre who was well acquainted with her work and with the spirit of Hispanic literature.

In 1940, Gabriela at her own request was transferred to Brazil, for she wanted above all to see to the safety of her nephew Juan Miguel, to whom she was devoted. She had asked Adelaida Portillo, who had a son of about the same age, to accompany her to Brazil and share her home, but her friend remained in Paris. As for Palma Guillén, she stayed in Switzerland until the beginning of 1942. Gabriela became consul first in Niteroi, Brazil, and then in 1941 in Petropolis, a picturesque mountain city, at an altitude of 800 meters and only 75 kilometers from Rio de Janeiro, to which she made brief visits. At first, Gabriela lived with her secretary Consuelo (Connie) Saleva from Puerto Rico, in a little house outside the city which she transformed into the peaceful Chilean Consulate, whose only adornment was the Chilean coat of arms. Later she bought a beautiful house in Petropolis itself. When she met Dominique Braga, her friend and colleague from the defunct International Institute of Intellectual Cooperation who had come to Brazil during the war, she invited him to see her new house and it was then she learned that the house she had just bought had once belonged to Count Francisco de Figueredo, the maternal grandfather of Dominique Braga. As a matter of fact, in the days of the Count, his six sons lived in Petropolis, each in a house of his own.

In spite of her apparent retirement and isolation, Gabriela contributed to the most important papers of Latin America, took an active part in the cause of the Allies, corresponded with Brazilian war protégés, fought against fascism, against hatred and the oppression of the Jews, and wrote poetry. She said in her poem "Emigrada judía" (The Immigrant Jew):

I am one looking back,
I am another facing the sea.
In my head farewells are throbbing,

and my heart is filled with anguish.
The rushing waters of my village
no longer speak my name in their froth
and my traces are erased from my land and
from the air
like steps on the sand. [115]

She was indefatigable in her constant struggle for a spiritual awakening and a closer relationship between Brazil and the Spanish-speaking countries.

In Brazil, she also wrote articles on Carolina Nabuco, Jorge de Lima, Asís Chateaubriand, and Renato Almeida, and on the close bond of language that should exist within the Ibero-American culture. She understood Brazilian writers and often said how indebted Chile and all of Latin America should be to Cecilia Meirelles, Henriqueta Lisboa, Ribeiro Couto, Renato Almeida, Oswald and Mário de Andrade, and many more for their translations of Spanish American poetry into Portuguese, and for the dissemination of Hispanic thoughts. In the same way, Gabriela stimulated interest in Brazilian literature among Spanish Americans, just as earlier Brazil had become known to Europe through the Ibero-American Collection of the International Institute of Intellectual Cooperation. Although Gabriela never belonged to the Brazilian literary circle which met in Petropolis on Saturdays during the summer at the Imperial Museum and which was presided over by Prince Dom Pedro, grandson of the Emperor, she was the friend of many of its members: Afrânio Peixoto, the distinguished Brazilian literary scholar, Tristão de Ataíde, the leading critic of that time, Dominique Braga and Stefan Zweig.

Gabriela was never alone, for people from various walks of life came to her. At one time, her great friend Hortensia do Rio Branco, the daughter of Brazil's former Minister of Foreign Affairs, stayed with her. Falconetti, the French actress from the Comédie Francaise, found a refuge for herself and her young son in Gabriela Mistral's home. Some of her many friends were Dominique Braga, who had founded in Petropolis the "Alliance Française" and was, together with Fedor Ganz, the literary guide of her nephew Yin-Yin, and Brazilian writers such as Renato Almeida, Cecilia Meirelles, Henriqueta Lisboa, Tasso da Silveira, Manuel Bandeira, Ribeiro Couto, Murilo Mendes, Jorge de Lima,

Gabriela Mistral, in New York in 1953.

Birthplace of Gabriela Mistral in Vicuña, Chile.

The Church of the Immaculate Conception
in Vicuña, where Gabriela Mistral was
baptized on April 7, 1889, the day of her birth.

Monte Grande, the beloved village of her
childhood, where she now rests.

Gabriela Mistral in 1897, at the age of eight.

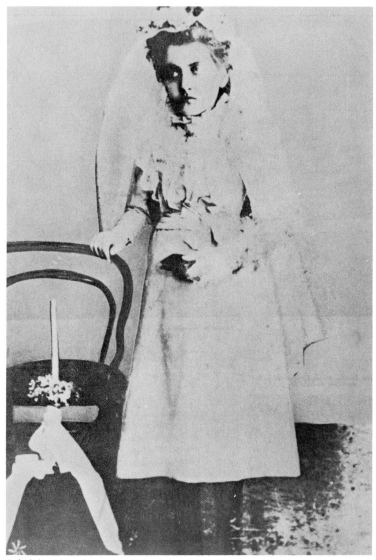

Gabriela Mistral on the day of her First Communion.

Gabriela Mistral as a rural schoolteacher in Chile.

Facsimile of Gabriela Mistral's signature.

Gabriela Mistral in 1930.

Gabriela Mistral during
a visit to Chile in 1938.

Gabriela Mistral surrounded by the children she so loved.

Gabriela Mistral receives the Nobel Prize for Literature from King Gustaf of Sweden on December 10, 1945.

Nobel Prize recipients. Left to right: Artùri Virtanon; Alexander Fleming; Ernst Chain; Gabriela Mistral, and Howard Florey.

Gabriela Mistral with President Truman during her visit to the
White House, on March 16, 1946. Standing are Don Marcial Mora
(left), Chilean Ambassador to the United States, and Humberto
Díaz-Casanueva, Counselor at the Chilean Embassy.

Gabriela Mistral
arriving at La Guardia
airport, New York, on
October 10, 1946.

Gabriela Mistral in New York in the 1940's.

Gabriela Mistral as she sailed for Chile on August 20,
1954, to be honored by her countrymen during the celebration of the Chilean National Holiday "El Dieciocho"
(Chilean Independence Day, the 18th of September).

Ceremony held at the United Nations on December 10, 1955 to commemorate the adoption of the Universal Declaration of Human Rights. From left to right; Gabriela Mistral, Dag Hammarskjöld, and Doris Dana.

Gabriela Mistral at work; she liked to use a board resting on the arms of her chair.

Gabriela Mistral with the author of this book, in Roslyn Harbor, New York, in 1956.

Gabriela Mistral, Roslyn Harbor, New York, in the last years of her life.

Sketch of Gabriela Mistral by the Chilean artist Jorge Délano. Courtesy Department of Public Information and Cultural Relations, Republic of Chile.

Children dancing in a round at the rhythm of her poetry put to music.

Graça Aranha, and Tristão de Ataíde. She also was in contact with the Jewish-Austrian exile and writer Stefan Zweig and many visitors from various countries such as Benjamín Subercaseaux, Waldo Frank, Roger Caillois, and Raymond Ronze. A small court always seemed to form around her, and in spite of her humility, she appeared to be a sovereign or a literary goddess who walked with an Olympian gait. Senhora Ribeiro Couto described to me Gabriela Mistral's white house before which her erect figure and her head stood out as if carved in wood or marble. Her conversations which sometimes lasted until sunrise were mostly about "her" Indians and reflected her constant curiosity about everything alive, which was an expression of her spirit of youth. In the course of a visit which I had with Ruy Ribeiro Couto in Paris, he recalled his friendship with Gabriela and said: "Gabriela links together all of Spanish America in a loving gesture which she extends toward Brazil. She is more than a poet, she is the symbol of Spanish America, she is a Bolívar. She stands for that which the Statue of Liberty represents in New York."

In February, 1941, Gabriela wrote a prologue to Benjamín Subercaseaux's book *Chile o una loca geografía* (Chile or a Crazy Geography), published by Ediciones Ercilla in Santiago, Chile, in 1942. In it she expressed her gratitude to the author, for in his book he had revealed his love of folklore and of the earth of his country: "I like the worshipping of the earth which is found in all folklore. Not only do I understand it, but I live it in its fullness. The earth was always the Great Idol, for it is the bountiful tray where all other adorations are embedded."[16] In an article published on August 30, 1943, in *El Mercurio* of Santiago, Benjamín Subercaseaux recalled her cordial and frank smile and her simplicity. During his stay in Brazil, he accompanied her on Mother's Day to a Brazilian School where she took part in the festivities and caressed the heads of the children as if recognizing each one of them through touch.

In 1942, under the initiative of the Carioca Academy of Letters of Rio de Janeiro, an article appeared in various papers of Central America which suggested that the Nobel Prize be awarded to Gabriela Mistral. However, the world was still heavy with war and tragedy and the awarding of Nobel Prizes had been interrupted. On February 23, 1942, Stefan Zweig, Gabriela's great friend, depressed by the state of the world and the fate of his people, the Jews, committed suicide, together with his young wife. He was sixty-one and she was thirty-three years old. This sudden tragedy made a very deep impression upon Gabriela and her friends. As early as 1935, Gabriela had written against the persecution of the Jewish people and throughout her life she was to defend their cause.

Stefan Zweig lived only a few blocks away from Gabriela. Ten days before, in their last encounter but one, he had spoken of the spiritual strength of their mutual friend Roger Martin du Gard, and had entered into a long conversation on the Indian, the Negro, and the people with mixed blood. He had also expressed the desire to receive in his home Waldo Frank, another common friend, who was arriving in Brazil, as well as to take a walk with Gabriela in the outskirts of Petropolis as they both shared a love for rural life. He considered Gabriela a great expert on plants, as he had seen her cultivate a portion of her garden with great care: "Gabriela Mistral, he told me, I have this wish that you must grant to me. We will converse about many things as we walk through the fields."[117]Stefan Zweig was a close friend of Brazil and had a deep understanding and knowledge of its people and its land: "All the nations mattered to him, but he had become very much attached to our people. . .he remained in Brazil and paid homage to it in his magnificent book about its territory, history, and nation."[118]A letter addressed to the President of the P.E.N. Club, Dr. de Souza, contained a farewell to his friends:

"Before leaving this life of my own free will and with a clear and sound mind, I feel the need to pay my last tribute to Brazil: It is imperative that I thank this marvelous country that has given me and my work a warm and hospitable refuge. Day by day I learned to love it more and I would not have wanted to find a new home anywhere else, now that the world of my mother tongue has vanished and that Europe, my spiritual homeland, has given in to self-destruction."[119]

Gabriela received the cruel news by a telephone call from Dominique Braga at 9 o'clock in the evening when she was already resting in bed and it was "Connie" (Consuelo Saleva), her secretary, who answered. In a letter written to Eduardo Mallea and later published in *El Mercurio,* Gabriela revealed how deeply she had been affected by the death of her friend: "There was nothing we could do for him, except give him our love. We loved him, the three of us, in this house because it was the most natural thing in the world to feel for him not only admiration, but also a deep tenderness. There was in him the sweetness of Isaiah, the flame of St. Paul, and the ambrosia of Ruth."[120]

The depressing years of war and the suicide of her friends were not the only blows Gabriela was to receive. On August 14, 1943, she suffered a personal tragedy in the sudden death of Juan Miguel, her nephew and the last member of her family. She had never had a personal life but gave herself unselfishly to all in need, and he had been her only comfort. Yin-Yin, as she called him, was a very intelligent and whimsical child who possessed a talent for writing and who had a French education. Fedor Ganz who tutored him in Latin recalled to me his great talents in the humanities. Yet Gabriela, in spite of being an educator, had hoped out of her love for nature and rural life that he would study agronomy. In 1943, he was a sensitive adolescent of about seventeen who had grown up among adults. He had shared Gabriela's roving life since about the age of four and looked up to Palma Guillén as a great friend and a second mother with whom he had remained at times for a few months and to whose advice he would listen. He was very close to Gabriela whom he often called "Buddha" because of her power of perception. He would walk beside her, be near her when she was sick; he would read to her and enrich her soul with his youthful conversations. Her nephew was more than a part of her life, he was her life itself, and his death shook her whole being, weakened her health and her desire to live. For nine days Gabriela was unable to move and for some time she remained in a state of prostration. She craved to see him in her dreams or while in vigil. Every day looked the same, without changes of seasons and colors. In November of that year she wrote: "He was the spirit of the house, he was the day, he was in every book. I know that God punishes harshly those who practice idolatry and by this I do not only mean the cult of images."[121]

The cause of his death remains in part a mystery. This much is known. He did not die a natural death, but was driven to take arsenic because of the cruelty of a group of fellow students who made his life unbearable in an atmosphere stifled by xenophobia. Perhaps because Yin-Yin had studied and lived in Europe the youths resented him and regarded him as a foreigner; perhaps also because he was related to a consul and an international figure, they envied him and hated him in spite of his warm and generous personality. He had brought them very often to the consulate. Perhaps, too, Yin-Yin, who was very sensitive, had been overimpressed by the suicide of Stefan Zweig and his wife. In a note of farewell, addressed to Gabriela, he wrote: "It is far better to die than to kill. Please forgive me, little mother."[122]He died five hours later in a hospital and although he struggled to live, he accepted death stoically. Gabriela was at his side during his agony: "I must go back to my old heresy and believe in the Karma of lives gone by to understand for what terrible crime of mine I am being punished at such a high price with the night of agony of my Juan Miguel. Such a frightful night in spite of the unbelievable stoicism with which he endured the blazing pain of arsenic in his dearly beloved body."[123]

Palma Guillén who immediately came to stay with Gabriela said that the years 1943-1945 she spent with her friend were the two saddest of Gabriela's life. While in Paris in 1946, Gabriela described to Adelaida Portillo through what anguish she had lived, and still later, in 1956, she often recounted to me in a vivid and moving way all the details of this tragedy. As Gabriela related in the letter quoted above, she turned to poetry, as she had done in her first book *Desolación,* to alleviate her pain and tried to find in it some of the elements of his beloved conversations: "Poetry was never for me something so strong as to enable me to replace this precious youth who spoke with the words of a child, a young boy, and an old man, and who never shut me out from his world. I have not the gift of oblivion to forget such a tragedy. It is braided in me and it swells in me every five minutes."[124] As she had once written vibrant poems in *Desolación* as an expression of her grief, she again created poignant verses in which she revealed the depth of her sorrow. However, these poems of mourning published in *Lagar* in 1954 were only related to the poems of her youth by their theme of death and love. They reflect a firm belief in eternal life and reveal a poetic form, purified and austere:

Once again I walk upon the earth
with a naked flank,
that poor raw flesh
where death comes swiftly
and my blood flows and rises
filling the vase to the brim.

. . . .

We walked silently
holding each other's hand,
and our blood would speak
with the same beat of our pulse.
Now, I carry lifeless
this right hand, this body.[125]

In the lapse of a night,
my sun fell, my day left,
and my flesh became like smoke
that a child slashes with his hand.

Colors faded from my clothes,
white and blue vanished
and I found myself one morning
a pine tree, smoldering in ashes.[126]

CHAPTER 3

Nobel Prize
and
Last Journey
Through
Life

*"I now hear the call of
Him who is my Master."*
GABRIELA MISTRAL

While Gabriela lived through her personal tragedy, the dawn
of peace lit up the world, and with that peace Stockholm began
to look again at Chile and at the poetry and work of the woman
who had sung the love of the weak and oppressed in her yearning for social justice. Already in 1941 an article by Ivan Harrie,
a critic of a Stockholm newspaper, had appeared in *El Mèrcurio,*
which said that Gabriela Mistral was a very probable choice for
the Nobel Prize: "One of the eighteen members of the jury has
made a sensational discovery in the contemporary Chilean literature: the poetess Gabriela Mistral who is introduced in *Bonniers
Littera Magasin* through a handful of poems, translated and com-
mented by Hjalmar Gullberg."[1]

On November 15, 1945, Gabriela Mistral's telephone in Petropolis rang constantly. She had received the Nobel Prize for Literature. It has been said that on hearing the news on the radio,
she knelt in front of the crucifix, that was always near her, and
that she humbly thanked God who had given her this honor as if
to alleviate her mourning. "Oh Lord, make your humble daughter
be worthy of such high laurels"[2] were her words. When the
Minister of Sweden in Brazil informed her that she had received
the Nobel Prize, she said: "I am grateful for the honor bestowed
upon Latin America."[3] This was the first Nobel Prize for Literature conferred upon Latin America and through Gabriela the voice
of Chile and of all the Hispanic world was not only heard but

recognized and acclaimed. Among the women who until then had been awarded the Nobel Prize were: the Swedish writer Selma Lagerlöf, to whom Gabriela Mistral had been compared; Sigrid Undset; Marie and Irène Curie; Grazia Deledda, and Pearl Buck.

Jacinto Benavente, the Spanish playwright who had received the Nobel Prize in 1922, spoke of Gabriela's recognition: "Gabriela deserves it more than anyone else. She had already made a name for herself through her unique pedagogical undertakings and her so tender and feminine poetry. We must all rejoice in this new triumph of Hispanic letters."[4] Victoria Ocampo said: "Through her, we listen to America."[5] Pablo Neruda, her compatriot who years later also won the Nobel Prize for Literature, rightly said of her when he was still a young poet:

"This mother without children seems to be the mother of every Chilean; her voice has questioned and praised all our native soil, from the cold forest range to the land of nitrate and copper. She has praised one by one the resources of Chile, from the impetuous Pacific Ocean to the leaves of the last southern trees. The small deeds and the small lives of Chile, stones and men, grains and flowers, snow and poetry have been praised by her very deep voice. She herself is like a part of our geography, regal and earthy, giving and mysterious."[6]

María Monvel wrote in *Poetisas de América* (Women Poets of Latin America): "Unique, absolute, complex, one, multiple, Gabriela Mistral is the greatest poet ever produced in Latin America and the greatest that ever wrote in the Spanish language."[7] Augusto Iglesias pointed out that women all over Latin America rightly saw in her triumph the Renaissance of the indigenous American race: ". . . Thousands of women in hundreds of schools witnessed in her triumph the rebirth of their native race. They saw a blossoming, in pale terra cotta, of the millennium of ancestral virtues, praised by someone who proclaims openly that she has her roots in the same copper-colored tree."[8]

Before Gabriela Mistral's departure for Sweden, the Chilean Ambassador to Brazil, Raúl Morales, accompanied by his wife, came to see her. He later said that she not only had been consul in Petropolis, but that she had carried out in that city and in Rio de Janeiro the work of cultural attaché by providing the Embassy with articles, interviews, and even newspaper clippings. However, in spite of her generous contribution, her natural modesty had not permitted the Ambassador to ask the Chilean Government that the title of cultural attaché be bestowed upon her.[9]

On November 18, Gabriela left for Stockholm on the Swedish liner "Ecuador," in a state of poor health. She was accompanied by María Terra, the wife of the nephew of former President. Terra of Uruguay. The Swedish press said of Gabriela on her arrival: "She possesses the exact appearance that you would want a poet laureate to have. She is tall and graceful, impressive and majestic. . . . Her face is a clear reflexion of the naked truth, which is at the core of her poetry."[10] On December 10, she received the Nobel Prize for Literature in the Philarmonic Palace "Konserthuset" from the hand of King Gustaf. Gabriela advanced with a majestic gait dressed in a velvet gown. This award was bestowed upon her "for the lyric quality inspired by the strength of her emotions which made her the symbol of Latin America's idealism."[11] Hjalmar Gullberg, a member of the Swedish Academy and the translator of Gabriela Mistral's poetry into Swedish, made a speech in which he gave the history and the legend of the "spiritual queen of all Latin America":

"You have made a long journey to be received by so short a speech. In the span of a few minutes, I have told, as a tale, to the fellow countrymen of Selma Lagerlöf, the remarkable pilgrimage which you have carried out from the pulpit of the school teacher to the throne of poetry. In paying homage to the flourishing Ibero-American literature, we address ourselves today most particularly to its queen, the poet of *Desolación,* who has become the great interpreter of compassion and of motherhood.

"I beg of you, Madame Mistral, to accept from the hands of His Royal Highness the Nobel Prize for Literature which the Swedish Academy has bestowed upon you."[12]

Gabriela Mistral showed her intense identification with the American continent; she did not speak in her own name, but in the name of the people and nations of Latin America. The Nobel Prize did not seem hers; it belonged to America. In her acceptance speech she said:

"Today Sweden turns toward far away Spanish America to honor it in one of its many craftsmen. The universal spirit of Alfred Nobel would be happy to include the Southern Hemisphere of the

American continent, which is so little known, in the radius of its work to preserve cultural life.

By a good fortune which never ceases to amaze me, I am at this moment the direct expression of the poets of Latin America and the indirect expression of the very noble Spanish and Portuguese languages. Both are pleased to have been invited to take part in Scandinavian life, with its folklore and its thousand year old poetry."[13]

After the ceremony she explained in an interview that she had not been nervous while receiving the Nobel Prize, for her thoughts had been with her deceased nephew whom she had loved as her own son.[14]

Gabriela remained in Sweden for a month and was honored by all the representative organizations and institutions of Sweden. She immediately won the heart of the Swedish people just as they had won hers. They saw in her another Selma Lagerlöf. Although she was invited to stay in Sweden as long as she wished, Gabriela went to France, Italy, and England where she had not been since before the war.

In 1946, she was the official guest of these countries. Although she was in poor health she traveled alone. In France, she was greeted at Le Bourget airport as a guest of the French Government and was made "Chevalier de la légion d'honneur." She was invited to stay at the Hôtel Bristol, but almost immediately moved to the apartment of one of her friends on rue du Cherche Midi. Mathilde Pomès had been designated by the Ministry of Foreign Affairs to accompany her in Paris to the various functions held in her honor, but she soon was surrounded by writers such as Aragon, Max Daireaux, and the Duchesse de La Rochefoucauld.

Even though Gabriela had once lived in France and for many years had worked at the International Institute of Intellectual Cooperation and had shared the life of many French writers, very little was known of her and all who met her were impressed by her simplicity. In an interview with *Les Lettres Françaises* in Paris, a reporter wrote: "She spoke very little of herself (and never did we see a more humble Nobel Prize winner), but a great deal about our Provence, the region she is so fond of because she lived in it for several years."[15]

M. Lecomte, appointed to receive her at the Society of Men

of Letters, knew very little about her and it was Mathilde Pomès who gave him the necessary·material for his speech, just as she had helped Paul Valéry with the information for the preface to *Poèmes choisis* (Selected Poems). In this book Mathilde Pomès stands out as a great interpreter of Gabriela's poetry. Originally prepared for publication before the war, it was finally issued in 1946. In the same year, another book translated by her friend Roger Caillois was published by Gallimard.

In Italy, she received the degree of Doctorate *Honoris Causa* from the University of Florence. She also had a beautiful and unusual audience with Pope Pius XII, during which she asked him not to pray for her, but for all the Indians of America who were her brothers. In later years she enjoyed recalling this event and spoke of it with emotion. Germán Arciniegas describes the meeting between the Pope and Gabriela:

"The Pope, she used to say, had never heard of these human beings lost in the solitude of the New World. He only knew about the elegance of the gigantic and European-like Buenos Aires. No one had ever spoken to him of those melancholy secret corners where centuries wither with the hope of a future illusion. According to Gabriela, this was an hour of friendship that left an indelible imprint on her memory, and it must also have been felt by the Pope. Gabriela was different from any other woman, she was truly exceptional. She cast a spell that bewitched. She used to say that, shortly after her audience with the Pope, he began a campaign in favor of the Indians of South America. He had not forgotten those creatures of God whom she had celebrated in her poetry."[16]

After a stay in England, Gabriela again left Europe for the United States. It was at Barnard College, New York, where she gave a lecture, that Doris Dana, who later became her fervent admirer, literary heir, and translator, heard her for the first time. Doris, who was a great follower of the German writer and philosopher Thomas Mann, had been asked by a friend to translate an article of Gabriela, "El otro desastre alemán" (The other German Disaster), for a book on Thomas Mann. Thus, the German writer became a link that brought the two women together.

Gabriela, who had been Chilean delegate to the United Nations Commission on the Status of Women since its creation, had also been appointed Consul of Chile in Los Angeles. She was then in poor health. She was suffering from hardening of the arteries and from diabetes, which at one time caused near blindness.

She remained as consul until 1948. As usual, she found solace in the countryside, this time in the small city of Santa Barbara. Her house on 729 Anapamú Street suited her taste. It was surrounded by trees, one of which was more than one hundred years old and Gabriela's pride. Later, when she lived in Italy, she would write to her friends in Santa Barbara asking them to take good care of her tree. It was more important to her than the house: "Everything I have is a house in California with two or three thousand books, and a one hundred year old husky tree. Please look after my good old tree."[17] Gabriela felt a great affection for the people of California; a profound friendship for these "happy people" as she called them. She often spoke to me about the kindness of the people of Santa Barbara who had helped her during her illness: "In California five neighbors took turns to take care of me without knowing who I was."[18] She would compare these people and the atmosphere created by them to the inhabitants of Provence and to those of her Valley of Elqui. She never thought that people knew about her because she had won the Nobel Prize. If I spoke of it to her she would laugh and would never refer to this honor by its name, only saying: "That thing from Stockholm."

In 1947, she went to New Orleans accompanied by Doris Dana who, by then, had become a close friend. Gabriela fell in love with the people of New Orleans whom she found so dynamic. Her feelings were reciprocated, and she was made, in her own words, an honorary daughter of the city.

At the invitation of President Miguel Alemán of Mexico, Gabriela went there with Doris in November, 1948. But upon reaching Yucatán, her health had a very serious setback and she almost died. Recalling her collapse years later, she wrote: "It lasted three hours. Everyone gave me up for dead. The whole town filled the hotel. I was saved by an American doctor who made the statement that the triple injection that he used, in the desperate attempt to save me, left my heart in a worse shape than before, that is to say, more crippled than before."[19] From that moment on, she felt a prisoner in her own house. Because of her heart

condition, she could not go to Mexico City, high in the mountains, in spite of her desire to see the school of San Angel where
she had once found peace and joy. However, she found new
friends and new homes in the states of Yucatán and Veracruz.
She lived for some time in Mérida, Fortín de las Flores, Orizaba,
and in the port of Veracruz itself. Two haciendas in Jalapa called
"El encero" and "La orduña" were placed at her disposal. The
haciendas were located near a village where there lived many Indians whom she so loved. Just as in 1922-24, she identified herself with them and helped them, and in this atmosphere, so close
to her spirit, she wrote much. Víctor Alba said of her: "And
her conversation is amusing and witty; she never puts on airs,
she does not talk about her work, nor does she theorize; she
only speaks out of profound conviction. She talks in the rural
language spoken by country women and she is fond of giving
nicknames to her friends, and she does this with much spirit,
without ever hurting anybody's feelings."[20]

Gabriela had come to Mexico as a guest of President Alemán
and the First Lady, Beatriz Velasco de Alemán, as well as the
poet Jaime Torres Bodet, then Director General of UNESCO.
She was to have stayed from three to six months, but she felt
so much at home there that she remained for two years as consul in Veracruz. She gave many lectures and devoted her time
to her friends, to the people of the villages who needed her help
and understanding, and to her own writing. Several writers and
artists came to see her from all over the country as she herself
could not travel; among them was the great Mexican writer Alfonso Reyes, who recalled for me his visits to Gabriela's rustic
house in Veracruz.

On Christmas Day, 1948, surrounded by a group of little ones
from a children's home, she spoke in Fortín de la Flores of the
closeness that exists between all the poor children of the American world and the Child Jesus. Her concept of Christianity was
one of social awareness and justice which made her see the face
of the Infant Jesus in each Indian, Negro, and mestizo:

"The child who sleeps in the frost and in the stormy snow drift
is not just an engraving made of plaster or a Christmas card.
Throughout the whole stretch of the Pacific, the Atlantic, and along
the Caribbean, I have seen with my own eyes the small Indian

child, the mulatto, the Negro and the mestizo sleep in such a way. And in spite of the geographic disparity, these native Latin American mangers all joined together around the Hebrew Cradle with the Mother of those denied lodging."[21]

It must be remembered that Gabriela was above all a rural school teacher and that her deepest love and interest since her fourteenth year had been directed toward the protection and defense of children.

In 1950, Gabriela returned to the United States. On December 12 of that year, she recorded some of her poems at the Library of Congress in Washington. It was also in Washington that she received the "Serra Award of the Americas" by the North American Academy of American Franciscan History. This pure and generous woman, who was a member of the Third Order of St. Francis, revealed in an address she delivered on that occasion a Franciscan simplicity so characteristic of her. Doris Dana, today her best interpreter in the English language, translated her speech:[22]

"The cord that we wear around our waist should remind us day by day, especially in time of strife, that our mission surrounds us and clings to us in the same way. . . .

"St. Francis lived through the struggles of the Middle Ages, but he was not caught up in their passion. He was a wanderer through all the roads of Umbria. . . .

"He felt near to the beasts, the birds, and the flowers. For him it was a most natural thing to befriend a wild animal, to protect the life of a bee, to converse with a falcon. When he sang his glowing tributes to the sun, to water, to fire, to all inanimate things, he desired only to show his kinship with the earth. This he considers somehow divine because our Lord Jesus Christ deigned to live on it when He came to regenerate us by His blood and His grace."[23]

Shortly afterward, Gabriela was again appointed consul in Italy and went to live in Rapallo, in a house surrounded by trees and facing the sea near the little beach of San Michele. Later, as consul in Naples, she lived at 220 Via Tasso. Her home attracted many Latin American visitors. She worked as an adviser to UNESCO. She had also been offered the directorship for South America of the United Nations International Children's Emergency Fund (UNICEF). She did not accept this position because of her delicate health and perhaps, too, because of her humble nature. Although she was not the official founder of UNICEF, she is considered its spiritual founder because she made the first worldwide appeal for its cause. An organization was also created in Rome to aid children born as a consequence of the invasion and Gabriela was appointed as its honorary president. Raoul Villedieu, Secretary General of the French Academy in Rome, was its president.

While Gabriela was consul in Naples, her friend Palma Guillén, who had a special commission in Rome, would either come to see her or invite her to Rome, and thus from time to time they spent eight to ten days together. When Palma was with her she would help her make selections of her prose works, or type them, so that they could be sent to a friend or to a magazine. As for her poems, Palma was always surprised to find them among papers or notebooks:

"Her poetry was always a surprise to me. I would find it lost, forgotten in a notebook that seemed unused, but suddenly, toward the middle, my eyes would fall upon some marvelous poems, or I would discover them on a sheet of paper left within the book she had been reading. I would carefully copy these first drafts and then one day I would place them in front of her so that she could read them or correct them. I still recall her light, dreamy or joyful eyes: 'It is not a bad work, Palmita. Leave it with me.' " [24]

Gabriela was driven constantly to revise her writing, seeking a pure form of art. This struggle for purity in form and expression is in many ways similar to that of the mystic in his step-by-step ascent to God. She submitted her art to tortuous doing and redoing. I remember, for instance, that in 1956 as I was reading aloud to her the poem "País de la ausencia" (Land of Absence), which had been published in *Tala* in 1938, she kept stopping me to change words and their order. Margaret Bates writes of Gabriela's constant correcting of her poems: "It was Gabriela's *modus operandi* in all her poetry. . .to correct her rough draft until the corrections began to menace legibility; the corrected draft would then be copied on a typewriter, this in turn would be corrected. The corrections would continue on subsequent copies until Gabriela felt she could no longer improve upon the poem."[25] Margot Arce de Vázquez notes Gabriela's continuous manipulation of her language in both her poetry and prose:

". . . We who have closely observed her create and elaborate poems and prose know how much care she gave to her words and expressions. We also know with what care she corrected and reworked what she had written, as she searched for an expression that would come close to the spoken language, that would have precision and the warmth of life and would correspond exactly to the mental image."[26]

As a writer, Gabriela knew the just balance between form and content. Style was not to her an end in itself. She was a poet concerned with beauty, but she also wrote with the purpose of bringing about reforms, of ameliorating man's lot. According to Palma Guillén, like the Romantics she used literature as a "social weapon."

Some of Gabriela's concerns expressed in her conversations and in her writings were the social status of Chilean women and children, the problems of education, and the struggles facing the young Chilean writers. She took a deep interest in the societies formed to help writers. As mentioned before, she helped the young who came to see her to discover the meaning of poetry and to search for basic themes in their reading. The only luxury that she indulged in was the great number of books that she constantly bought; she would give them generously to her numerous friends, young and old, speaking to them for example of the great value of the Greek classics and of the works of the Italians, in particular Dante, to whom she affectionately referred as "My Father Dante." For many years she had sent money, and clothing for the children of her Valley of Elqui in her desire to maintain a feeling of closeness. She also sent many worthwhile books to a Spanish friend, Pedro Moral, so that she could help enlarge the library of Vicuña, which bore her name, and enrich the minds of the children she loved. When she received the "Chilean National Prize for Literature" in 1951, she asked that the proceeds of the Prize be distributed in her name to the children of the Valley. Senator Radomiro Tomic, accompanied by other officials of the government, brought the Christmas message of Gabriela to the children and the people of Elqui and all felt deep emotion at the distribution of the clothing and books sent by the faraway friend whose name was almost magic there. Some of these touching scenes were described to Gabriela who was still in Italy:

"Our first stop was at the house in which you were born. We were received by a friend of yours, who was your devout admirer and who moved us with these words: 'My only desire is to see Gabriela; I would not mind dying after this.' The senator remarked: 'What magic one must have to incite such enthusiasm.' "[27]

The official ceremony of awarding her the Chilean National Prize for Literature took place on December 4, 1951, in Gabriela's absence, in the Municipal Theatre of Santiago. Her literary and spiritual contribution to Chile was at last unanimously recognized: "We Chileans have always felt Gabriela Mistral close to us, bound to us by a restless love for our land and its destiny, which she embodies and proclaims to the world through her poetry and the exemplary nobility of her whole being." [28]

Her love of Chile and of children was so much a part of her that it formed the essence of *Poema de Chile* (Poem about Chile), the long narrative poem she was writing up to the time of her death and which was published in 1967. This last work stands as poetic praise of her country: its fruits, flowers, woodlands, mountains and sea, its people and its birds and animals. It is an exaltation of her country toward which her thoughts traveled constantly, re-creating from memory every region, every animal, every plant in its smallest detail. In *Poema de Chile,* she returns to Chile as a spirit after death, only visible to a little Indian boy from Atacama—the region from which her father came—and a little baby fawn. With them she wanders over every region of Chile, singing to them of a beauty they cannot understand by themselves: the Northern Pampa, the green patches of the North (the fertile Valley of Elqui), the farmland of the central region, the depth of the forests in the southern part of Chile, the rivers, the sea, and the Cordillera Mountain. Together they pass quickly over the cities as did Cervantes throughout the adventures of his Don Quixote for, he too, could only find solace within the tranquillity of nature. The child would like to pick the flowers, but Gabriela tells him that they are there to behold as a feast for the eyes. The verb "to stop" comes up very often, for it means that Gabriela, the little boy, and the baby fawn must pause in their discovery of nature. This is the reason why they try to avoid houses and people. Taking the little boy by the hand, she stops to admire the friendliness of nature, the simple beauty of the grass, roots, and flowers, and she teaches him the names of everything they see:

> *Why do plants still matter to you, why?*
> *My little one, I was a gardener.*
> *My mother passed this love down to me.*
> *We would go through the fields*
> *in search of fruits and herbs that heal.*
> *I asked her as we walked along*
> *the names of trees and bushes*
> *and she knew them all*
> *With their virtues and their tricks.*[29]

Gabriela converses with the child, answers his questions, speaks to him of the flora and fauna of Chile, explores with him the geography of her country. At times she plays with him, at times the child and the deer talk together. Their common sense contrasts with the poetic philosophy of Gabriela's spirit.

But *Poema de Chile* is not just a conversation with a little boy and his adventures across Chile. It is a dialogue between Gabriela Mistral, the poet, and Lucila Godoy, the little girl she once was, and their reunion as they discover together the many hidden beauties of their country. Gabriela tells the little boy that as a child she had established a dialogue with God's creatures and was more at ease with them than with other twelve-year old girls who knew the practical side of life and could sew, cook, and wash dishes. At every step, something about Gabriela is disclosed, her love for music, her sadness at not being able to sing, and the joy and consolation she found in poetry. Like St. Francis she is fond of giving everything an affectionate name; the sea becomes a father, the mountain, a mother. The wind, she says, has many names and she took one of them as her pseudonym:

> *I found it in foreign lands,*
> *hard, playful, violent,*
> *Women feared it*
> *like the evil spirit of fairy tales;*

it swept my soul away,
it strengthened my breath
and rejoiced my song.[30]

Gabriela was a perfectionist; she liked to write about what she knew well. For that reason, she collected all the information she could gather about the various regions of Chile. She would write to her friends asking for some small detail about a bird or a plant, but would often not receive the answer that she needed. In her conversations with people who came to see her, she always found a way of speaking of Chile, and was sometimes disappointed upon finding that they did not know anything about nature. She also read every book written about Chile and collected those with illustrations about Chilean life. She had always had a great liking for books that taught geography, zoology, and botany through drawings, engravings, and photographs. During the last five years of her life, she collected such books with illustrations of birds, animals, and plants with texts written in French, English, or Spanish. They gave her enjoyment and at the same time helped her:

"I have a visual memory and the few pictures that I have of Chile move me, delight me, and help me."[31] "All these things are helpful to me. Sometimes a single picture is more useful to me than a whole treatise, and a popular song has more impact than a history of literature."[32]

Actually, the visual and tactile senses played a very important part in her art. She very often described a person or a landscape as if she were a painter, and she also knew how to touch as if she were a sculptor. In her articles or in her conversations, she gave special importance to physical attributes, for example, a writer's looks and his voice. Several of her articles are called "portraits." Gabriela also liked to collect ceramic, metal, or wooden animals—mostly deer. This was another luxury, like her purchase of books. She was fond of choosing them herself and would refer to her going out in search of photographs, reproductions, and statuettes as *"salir de monería"* (going trinketing). She affectionately gave the name of *"monos"* (trinkets) to any illustration of plants and animals.

In 1953, Gabriela Mistral was invited by the Cuban Government to participate in the celebration of José Martí's centennial.

She was accompanied on her trip by an American friend, Margaret Bates, whom she had met in Rome and to whom she had given the nickname of "Niña de Roma" (The Young Girl from Rome). She remained during her stay at the home of the Cuban writer Dulce María Loynaz, who introduced her to the Ateneo of Havana. The Cuban people were grateful to Gabriela for her own acknowledged indebtedness to Martí and for the poems and prose articles she had written about Cuba. She had said during her first trip to Cuba in 1922; "The nearing of foreign shores has been something very sweet, like the infant who nears his mother's breast, which he had left for an instant. And this is the impression I have of Cuba. Havana, where one does not know what is best: the sea or the bread."[33] A throng of people surrounded her constantly, many out of curiosity; they did not realize that she longed greatly for solitude. She, nevertheless, found solace in a favorite place, near the fountain of Dulce Maria Loynaz's garden, where she would drink with pleasure many cups of tea.

On her return from Cuba, Gabriela spent a month in Florida and then went to New York. As Chilean delegate to the United Nations Commission on the Status of Women, she represented Chile at the seventh session, held from March 16 to April 3, 1953, as well as during the eighth session, from March 22 to April 9, 1954.

She lived briefly in the city before moving to Roslyn Harbor, Long Island, with her friend Doris Dana. The house was surrounded by flowers, the bay windows looked out on a little wood. Gabriela had a great love for trees, mountains, and the sea. She once said to me in speaking of a tree: "He looks like a King." It was in this peaceful atmosphere that she continued writing and correcting her narrative *Poema de Chile.* During my visits with her, she would read some pages of her poem in a voice that was almost a psalmody; then, looking into my eyes, she would smile, as if amused by her own poetry or by the thought of reading it to me or as if she had been caught reading someone else's poetry.

Gabriela never cared for her own voice which she thought monotonous, and she was almost apologetic when she read aloud. Actually, her voice did have a certain rhythm with a touch of sadness and lassitude, but it also had a captivating magic to it. As a teacher, when she put aside her notes and her books, she would improvise the most beautiful words on what seemed to others ordinary topics: trees took on a human aspect; the window pane became unique in its own way; the grass breathed; the rock felt. When she taught about raw materials in a school for workers, she would tell them stories that showed the wonder of iodine, chalk, or salt. Whether through poetry or through her own art of storytelling, Gabriela made the four elements, air, earth, water, and fire, her intimate and vital friends. She once said that she had divided themes into those that had a halo around them and those that did not, but that she soon came to realize that each one had something supernatural that she had not perceived at first. Gabriela was fascinated by storytellers and she could improvise on any theme although she was never able to write a short story. She always held to the belief that teaching ought to be complemented by the art of storytelling.

Her language, like that of the storyteller, evokes all the forms and qualities of an oral message, direct, warm, and colorful; this language was nourished by the folklore of the Valley of Elqui and by that found in the Bible. Those who listened to her, in spite of what she said of her own voice, were left under her bewitching spell.

In 1954, Gabriela gave several lectures at the University of New Orleans. She also attended an international festival of writers in Pittsburg, organized by Pedro Labarthe, where she read portions of her *Poema de Chile.*

In August, 1954, she sailed on the steamship "Santa María" accompanied by Doris and arrived in Chile on September 5 after sixteen years of absence. She had come at the invitation of the then President of Chile, Carlos Ibáñez, as a guest of honor of the Chilean Government. Just before her arrival, on September 3, a new edition of *Desolación* had been published by Editorial del Pacífico in Santiago.

The welcome that awaited her everywhere was very moving. She landed in Valparaíso, the chief port of Chile and one of the cities she liked most. A special train waited there to bring her in triumph to Santiago. Oscar Herrera, the Minister of Education, Major Santiago Polanco, the President's military aide-de-camp, Hernán Díaz Arrieta (Alone), a well-known critic and personal friend of Gabriela, and many others escorted her to the capital. Thousands of children, men, and women—teachers, laborers, young and old—had gathered at each stop of the train to see her—in Viña del Mar, Limache, Quillota, La Calera—singing her poems put to music. Gabriela received these tributes from the window of the railway car, stretching her hands to the children and repeating with visible emotion: "How healthy and handsome are the children of my land. I shall come back to see them and chat with them. I shall visit them in their schools or in their homes."[34] Acknowledging the welcome rendered to her in the name of the city by its Mayor, Gabriela expressed her joy at having returned to Chile: "I am happy, very happy, to set foot once again on Chilean soil. One of my greatest dreams was to arrive at Santiago, to be united once more with my people, with you, and this dream has come true."[35]

In an open car that took her to the Palace of La Moneda, she rode along Alameda O'Higgins, the principal avenue of Santiago, where thousands of people were waiting for her. Gabriela passed under an arch of triumph made of flowers, bearing the inscription: "He who sows well sows happily," children sang her *"rondas infantiles"*[36] and students from all the high schools of Santiago were present, and tossed flowers as she passed. Gabriela and her retinue arrived at the presidential palace where President Ibáñez and members of the government awaited her. From one of the balconies, Chancellor Roberto Aldunate, presenting her to the people gathered in front of the palace, said: "I leave her with you, the people, who are eager to listen to her,"[37] and Gabriela among many things spoke these words: "I was never happier than when I found out that all the peasants had their own patches of land."[38] She did not realize her own importance; she spoke not of herself, but of her joy in seeing her own people—the laborers and the peasants— happy. She spoke in a familiar tone, as an old teacher to her children:

"I am very grateful to you for having accompanied me here. It is an honor for me and an intense joy to see that my beloved people have felt the strong ties that bind their old teacher with you all. I have never forgotten this link. I let you go now so that you may rest. We shall soon meet at your work or in your own homes. I would like to give you all the time I have; but I must tell you with regret that my strength has lessened. But my good will is not small. I am a Chilean who has been away, but I am not an absentee.''[39]

Among the many honors bestowed upon her was the Degree of Doctorate *Honoris Causa* which she received from the University of Chile on September 10, 1954. In an inspiring acceptance speech, she spoke of the role of the intellectual and of the teacher, whose duty should go beyond their work in an endeavor to help the needy and create a communion of spirit between the city and the country:

"The professional man as well as the artist must not only become aware of the man and woman whose lives are a long and vast purgatory, he must offer them his friendship. Because poverty that turns into utter misery in certain works and under the effect of harsh climates, of extreme cold or heat, is like a purge that does not make the body healthy, nor helps the soul; it irritates or makes man dull and unfeeling out of sheer boredom. I said 'friendship' but I could simply have used the word 'help' because it is a matter of giving out assistance or a comforting presence. The educated man is almost always a strong creature and therefore capable of consoling. Material resources may be limited, but those of the spirit are more powerful than we could ever imagine and those that have the upper hand in any circumstance shall be the strongest.''[40]

Gabriela read only a part of her speech because upon reaching the last page of her notes, she saw she had left the rest of it at home. In an informal way, so typical of her, she exclaimed: "I have left the rest at home. I have behaved like a forgetful child. Please forgive me. I would like, with the Rector's permission, to speak to you.''[41] Improvising, she talked movingly for one hour to the large audience as if she were among a few intimate friends. She related her impressions of various European countries—Italy, Belgium, Denmark; expressed her deep interest in the economic and cultural rise of the rural people; recounted various anecdotes of her life in different regions of Chile and her love for Punta Arenas and the southernmost tip of Chile. She spoke of the future of her country, of agrarian reforms, of ways of combating misery, and asked the audience about the present-day life of the miner, whose cause she had always defended. Doris Dana had to interrupt her after an hour, because

Gabriela had so completely forgotten herself in her preoccupation with the well-being of her people that she would have collapsed from exhaustion had she continued. This was a most beautiful and unforgettable experience to hear the names of miners and peasants pronounced within the academic walls of the University; an unusual, informal talk for those who had expected a sophisticated speech; but a most natural monologue for Gabriela who had come back to Chile, not to talk about herself or about her work, but to question the people about the fate of those for whom she cared most, to be reassured that social progress was not just a word, but an integral part of life.

Gabriela remained in Chile for over a month. She received the honors of the State and was declared an illustrious guest of all the cities, in each of which she was given a medal. In Santiago, she stayed with the family of her friend, Radomiro Tomic, at Las Torcazas 242. Reminiscing about Gabriela's trip, Dr. Tomic said:

"She did us, Chileans, the great favor of revealing to us in a sensitive way our essential traits. At every port, the docks were crowded with people from all walks of life; the songs of thousands of children, beneath the balcony of the Mayor's residence in Valparaíso; the slow passing of the presidential train on its way to Santiago and the swelling intensity exploding as the convoy passed through each town or village;. .men and women teachers, thousands of children, paper banners, children singing in a round profiled in the distance, vibrating at the motion of the train, then dissipated suddenly in the midst of a verse, as the train continued on its way; the flow of a hundred thousand people in Santiago who rushed to see her, even from a distance, in spite of the general transportation strike.

"A strange alliance between her people and that sad woman. . .; that woman upon whom rested so heavily the hand of God; whose inspiration as well as her life is pierced by an only cry, a penetrating and desolate cry, and for whom during the dawn, noon, and twilight of her life, children and the poor were the supreme object of her love and her friendship."[42]

The tribute that probably moved her the most was to see that in Santiago, despite a bus strike that had paralyzed the whole city, 45,000 children had managed to come to hear her at the

National Stadium. This was the greatest homage that could be rendered to a teacher, and Gabriela was above all a teacher. She loved children and children loved her and learned through her poetry to spell and to read as well as to sing. Facing those thousands of children, Gabriela was happy and she talked to them as if she were a mother talking to her own children: "I am not going to make a long speech. I see over there a group of young girls without stockings. I do not want them to catch cold."[43]

Gabriela had become the greatest symbol of her people, she was the "spiritual queen of all Latin America" as Hjalmar Gullberg had so rightly called her at the ceremony awarding her the Nobel Prize. She had become almost a prisoner of her fame, for she was invited to one place after another and had interview after interview, which left her little time to herself. How she would have liked to be able to collect vital material for her *Poema de Chile,* to have time to reflect and meditate upon it, to visit with workers in their homes and children in their rural schools. How, too, she would have liked to remain in Monte Grande, enjoying the peace and quiet that an unknown person could have had. She had foretold in 1952 how as an official guest she would have little chance of intimate contact with Chilean nature: "If I go to Chile, would I see my homeland? I don't think so. I would be taken from one place to another as an official guest, without any privacy. This is the drawback of fame."[44] It would have suited her better not to stay in the capital, but in Valparaíso, and from there to make trips throughout the country:

"I respectfully ask of my superiors that they grant me, if possible, the pleasure of dwelling in Valparaíso or in its outskirts during my stay in Chile. From there I can go up to my Valley of Elqui or down to Punta Arenas. This is my wish, but it is also my debt toward these places. As I shall pass through the southern provinces and through my own, I will be pleased to talk with my people and to gather the material on Chilean flora that I need for a long narrative poem which I am writing about Chile."[45]

In October 1954, Gabriela was back in New York. At the end of the same month, she received the Degree of Doctorate *Honoris Causa* from Columbia University on the occasion of the University's bicentennial. Among the forty-eight recipients of honorary degrees were the Queen Mother of England, Adlai Stevenson, Konrad Adenauer, and Dag Hammarskjöld. *The New York Times* wrote on that occasion: "Early a teacher in the rural schools of her native Chile; renowned poetess, the beauty of whose *'Desolación,'* in 1922, made the world of letters her province;. . .recipient in '1945 of the Nobel Prize for Literature; an illustrious woman."[46]

From that time until her death, Gabriela lived in Roslyn Harbor, Long Island. On December, 1954, the Editorial del Pacífico of Santiago published her book *Lagar* (Wine Press) the result of sixteen years of writing, the span of years since *Tala,* her book published in 1938. In gratitude for the warm and vibrant welcome of her people, she offered Chile the only thing she could give: her book. It was said of *Lagar:* "In the poems that are included in this new book—the first one that Gabriela allows to be published in a long time—the readers of *Desolación* will notice a new tone and a different poetic form, naked and more austere, that at times reaches a classic and solemn purity of lines."[47]

Lagar is a synthesis of all her thoughts and emotions: her concern for all those who suffered, the Jews persecuted by racial hatred, nations being destroyed during the Second World War, the prisoners and the sick who were left alone with no one to care for them; it is also, as in *Tala,* a song to the Latin American continent, with its trees, mountains and sea, with its Indians, and with the magic hands of workers; as in *Ternura,* a music that lulls children and grownups; and as in *Desolación,* an outburst of passion as she came face to face with the death of her young nephew. *Lagar* discloses many autobiographical traits. It is the mature Gabriela who looks at life and who prepares for death. It is at the same time a discovery and a farewell. Her thoughts and her style take on a parallel expression: pure, concise, in one breath concrete and abstract, body and soul. Gabriela had waged a war against a part of herself and the spirit within her had won. She had subdued her strong ego and drawn closer to God. As she was preparing for this journey toward Him, she began to detach herself from the world. In her poems "La otra" (The Other) and "El costado desnudo" (The Naked Flank), she wrote:

> *One within me I have killed:*
> *one I did not love.*
> *She was the burning flower*

of the mountain cactus;
she was dryness and fire
she never quenched her thirst.[48]
I walked each breath
toward an approaching eternity,
without the burden of the tardy,
with this, my second body,
corroded by iodine and salt,
that goes straight from Gaea to God
like a dart,
as light and sharp
as the edge of my flank.[49]

On December 10, 1955, Gabriela was invited to participate in the concert held in honor of the seventh anniversary of the Proclamation of the Universal Declaration of Human Rights at the United Nations. She attended the concert seated between her great friend Dag Hammarskjöld and Doris Dana, but she did not read the message she had prepared for the occasion, perhaps because she was too tired to do so or perhaps because of her accustomed modesty. It was read by José Maza, a Chilean, then President of the General Assembly of the United Nations:

"Eight years ago, two words were given to the peoples of many nations and millions of mankind, and it is those words that we celebrate today in the form of Human Rights.

"Many countries had already been so favoured, but it was not the whole of mankind that enjoyed these rights. At last the day arrived, eight years ago, and we celebrate it as the birth of an era.

"There were not a few who doubted that freedom would bring well-being for the backward peoples and had themselves withheld this just favour from both men and women. We celebrate the universal nature of your achievement in the cause of civilization, yet there is still a note of sadness in our celebration. A glance round the world will leave us thoughtful.

"On this day, we remember this vast and noble achievement and fervently express the hope that this date will be a most glorious one in the calendar of 1956.

"The chosen ones that received the divine spark did not come down to redeem the multitudes alone; they came to save all peoples who should come after.

"We of the present day who are weary of this long waiting, who are unwilling to continue to live as privileged beings, will pursue this campaign. In no sacred writings is there anything resembling privilege, still less discrimination, two things that humiliate and insult the human person. I should be happy if your noble effort to secure human rights were taken up in complete good faith by every nation in the world. That would be a triumph transcending everything achieved in our time."[50]

On February 18, 1956, Gabriela was the guest of honor at a meeting of the Pan-American Women's Association held in New York in honor of Chile. I had been chosen by her to recite some of her poetry which she had selected. Her thoughts were thus reflected in the reading of "La huella" (The Footprint), a poem that expresses her desire for justice; "La Cordillera," an almost humanized description of the Andes Mountains; and "País de la ausencia" (Land of Absence), a summation of the memories of various countries she had known. On April 15, she also attended a meeting of the Pan-American Union in Washington, where some of her poems were read. On one or two occasions she also went to Princeton to see her old friend and spiritual brother, Jacques Maritain. For the most part, however, she remained in Roslyn Harbor, seeing a few friends, writing poetry, taking care of the flowers in her garden, talking with her cats—a Siamese called "Pussywillow" and its offspring, "Negrito," a big black cat and Gabriela's favorite.

Often during winter days, even though she awoke at 6 A.M., Gabriela would remain in bed while she worked. Her room became a study, many books and newspapers were scattered upon her bed, and she would read them conscientiously as if she were a student, underlining with colored pencils passages that she felt important. Negrito would rest comfortably among the books after he had had an adventurous night in the gardens of Roslyn. In this familiar atmosphere, Gabriela corrected and continued writing her *Poema de Chile* and the second part of *Lagar,* and also made some changes in the already published poems of *Desolación* and *Lagar.* Sometimes she would sit in the living room, using as a desk a board that rested on the arms of her chair, writing poetry or letters to her friends. These letters were like interrupted conversations, in which she told of the books she had been reading, the friends she had just seen, the discussions she had had. Gabriela seldom read novels, but gave most of her time to biographies, poetry, and philosophy. She often spoke, for example, of the greatness of Henri Bergson. She would say to me: "One should read much and especially every day." She had read the Bible many times, underlining with colored pencils what at the moment appealed to 'her most. She was fond of rereading the books that she greatly admired.

On warm days, Gabriela like to sit or walk in her garden or water the roses, talking to them as if they were little children. She also enjoyed going for rides in the car, planning new trips that she knew she could not undertake; visiting several houses that she knew she would never buy, just for the sake of driving through the countryside. She called herself *"patiloca"* (itchy feet) for she was fond of moving around. She once wrote: "I do not deny that I am a wanderer. The world is a beautiful place and perhaps when I am dead I will not be able to walk about it as I would like to."[51]

Because of her love for children, she was also fond of visiting schools where she would point out to the young the importance of discovering one's vocation in life, a theme that was very close to her. On one occasion, Doris recounted to me, a little boy unexpectedly asked Gabriela how she had found her vocation. Gabriela's answer, just as unexpected, was: "My little one. . .I I have missed my true calling. . . .I would have liked to become a chemist." She was attracted to what was concrete, what was real.

In November, 1956, Gabriela was first taken to the Flower and Fifth Avenue Hospital, in New York, and it was then that the doctors learned that she was suffering from cancer. However, Doris was not told this news until the end of December, and Gabriela never found out about it. In her room were flowers sent by Dag Hammarskjöld. Learning of her illness, he wanted her to know that he was thinking of her even if he could not see her because of his many responsibilities.

After a few days in the hospital, Gabriela returned to Roslyn. Upon hearing about the decline of her health, President Carlos Ibáñez had written to her, asking if she wanted to return to Chile. Shortly afterwards, she entered Hempstead General Hospital in

Long Island. She thought it was a sign of weakness or childishness to be carried to the ambulance and she insisted upon walking. The nurses were so impressed by her fortitude that one of them, a Latin American, gave her a present. It was a very large doll that was placed on a chair near her bed. During that short stay in the hospital, Gabriela spent some of her time reading her biography by Augusto Iglesias, *Gabriela Mistral y el modernismo en Chile* (Gabriela Mistral and Modernism in Chile), published in Santiago in 1949. It entertained her and she read it conscientiously as if it were not about her. She also listened to Italian music, to old Hebraic-Spanish songs such as "Sefardita española," the Psalms of King David, and the "Song of Solveig" by Grieg.

Among the visitors she received were her Spanish friend Victoria Kent; Germán Arciniegas, the Colombian writer and then professor at Columbia University; Victoria Ocampo, her Argentine friend who was so depressed by Gabriela's illness that she could only stay a few minutes. One day, when I was with her, Germán Arciniegas came with his daughter Gabrielita, and after he had answered her many questions about conditions in Latin America, a matter that always preoccupied her, he spoke to her of Hungary and asked whether she would sign a petition in defense of the Hungarian revolution. She did so. In spite of her illness, Gabriela remained the same generous hostess, forgetting at times that she was in the hospital. She wanted her guests to be well taken care of, offered them tea, and was almost conquettishly sorry to receive them in bed. She kept her good humor at all times and said of her hospital room that it had been made for millionaires.

Then she returned once more to Roslyn where she seemed to be feeling better. It was during those days of apparent improvement that her great friend Jacques Maritain, the former French Ambassador to the Vatican, a great Catholic philosopher and writer and then professor at Princeton University, came to see her. They spoke together for a long time of God, life, and death, all the religious questions that were so close to both their hearts.

On December 29, Gabriela was again taken to Hempstead General Hospital. This time she was in a different room, on the fourth floor, but still looking out at big trees, under the snow. I saw her on what was perhaps the last conscious day of her life. She was sitting up in bed, and she smiled as I came in, holding my hand long in her own hands. On a table by her side were the picture of her mother that she always kept with her and a cruci-fix which was to accompany her to the Life Beyond. She spoke of her mother, as if already with her in spirit. She seemed far away, near her mother and those she had loved. I felt as if her mother were standing by her side, just as I was, and at that very moment I understood that the visible and invisible worlds had touched and had become one. From the window could be seen a beautiful sunset. When I left her in the evening, she again pressed my hands in hers and with her warm and human smile she said: "We will see each other on Tuesday." Yet she must have known she was going to die. She thought she suffered from diabetes and from a weak heart.

On January 2, she asked to receive extreme unction and twenty-four hours later she fell into coma and never regained conscious-ness. The Papal blessings had also been given to her by the Chilean Jesuit, Father Renato Poblete of Santiago. On January 10, 1957, at 4:18 A.M., she died after a long struggle. She was 67. She died of cancer of the pancreas.

Gabriela had at last reached the peace she had much wished for, she had known the truth, had been assured of life after death, had seen the Gates of Heaven, had seen everything grow brighter and brighter. Once before, when she had almost died in Yucatán, she had the beautiful experience of seeing a circle of light. Her last word was "Triumph." Doris was near her and saw her reach that state of spiritual exaltation.

Her will expressed her wish to be buried in Monte Grande, the humble village of her youth, surrounded by green hills in the interior of the Province of Coquimbo. In her love for her people, Gabriela had asked that the proceeds from the sale of her books published in Latin America be placed in the custody of the Order of St. Francis for the benefit of the poor children of Monte Grande. Doris Dana, her friend and spiritual daughter, was left as her literary executrix. Gabriela bequeathed to Chile the gold medal and the citation of the Nobel Prize.

On January 10, the General Assembly of the United Nations interrupted its debate on Hungary to honor the memory of the emi-nent Chilean poet. The Chairman of the Chilean delegation, Am-bassador Roberto Aldunate, said:

"Gabriela Mistral's voice with its deep pacifistic quality was heard throughout the world. Wherever she went, on a lecture, in literary events, in student gatherings, at schools, on the University platform, and even on the podium of the United Nations, she spread abundantly the seeds of peace calling on the minds of people to overcome all limiting passions in order to reach a universalism that would allow all of us to understand one another.

"Her words were always an invitation for every human being to love, to overcome himself, to leave behind everything that is petty and negative within himself.

"Gabriela Mistral is to be counted among great fighters because of the extent of her spiritual understanding that brings down barriers between men. She belongs to the same moral standard as the best known universalists such as Romain Rolland or Hermann Hesse in Europe, or Ramakrishna or Gandhi in India.

"For this reason, in this Assembly where one struggles daily for the preservation of peace, I have brought to you her image now that her body is about to be totally surrendered to the earth."[52]

In the United Nations General Assembly's Social, Humanitarian and Cultural Committee, the Chilean delegate René Montero paid tribute to Gabriela Mistral and was joined in this eulogy by spokesmen from more than twenty delegations. Hermod Lannung of Denmark, the Chairman of the Committee, offered his deep sympathy to the Chilean nation and people. Benjamín Cohen of Chile, Under-Secretary for Trusteeship, expressed the irreparable loss for Chile and for the world of letters in the death of so great a woman: "I feel intensely her death and, united with all the Chileans of the United Nations Secretariat, I bow before her mortal remains with the fervent admiration and love that will surround her return to her native land, the land to which she brought so much honor as a superior woman and as its representative."[53]

Víctor Andrés Belaúnde, Gabriela Mistral's old colleague from the League of Nations, then Chairman of the Political Committee of the General Assembly, expressed his feelings in these words:

"Gabriela Mistral was the great poet of Latin America. She molded in her strong and simple verse the maternal feeling of women. Her social emotion was the reflection of her deep Christian charity.

"Her prose was as beautiful as her poetic form. Perhaps it could have been said of her what was affirmed of Valéry: that if his poetry was of gold, his prose was of diamond.

"A sense of mystery, a Christian love, a maternal attitude in women, a cult of the pure and rigorous forms of the language, a love for solidarity within Latin America, united to its Hispanic and Latin roots."[54]

Alfredo Hernández, Cuban Consul in New York, spoke in the name of the diplomatic corps of the Latin American republics and of Spain as follows: "We have come as the expression of mourning of all our nations that together with Chile have felt the sorrow of being dismembered in the loss of the great Gabriela: we unite with the people of Chile in this hour of tribulation, and we feel that through her death we have lost something essential."[55]

The Chilean Francisco Aguilera, then Assistant Director of the Hispanic Foundation in the Library of Congress, said: "As a fellow countryman and as her friend since the time we both lived in Chile, I can only say that her death will deeply affect all of us who live far from our homeland. She set an example for all of us. We were always guided by her."[56]

José A. Mora, Secretary General of the Organization of American States, also said: "We, the people of the Pan-American Union, feel profoundly enriched by her poetry and her warm and stimulating personality. We mourn her death, but we also know that she shall always continue to live in her poetry, for her poems are her legacy to humanity."[57]

Lincoln White expressed on behalf of the State Department of the United States the grief of his country: "The Government of the United States shares, with the Government of Chile and its people, the loss of this beloved personality in the field of the arts."[58]

Numerous people, both humble and well known, gathered to pay their last respects at her funeral in New York. Among them were the Mayor of New York, Robert Wagner, the diplomatic corps of countries from all over the world and many personal friends.

I, who had been close to her, knew that she was no longer there, that this inert and frail body was only the envelope that had contained her soul. This could not be Gabriela for she was real, she was part of life. Her piercing blue-green eyes, her warm smile, almost childlike and mischievous, were now in our own hearts. Speaking of her great friend, Doris Dana later imparted to me words of consolation, Gabriela's message: "Gabriela taught us a lesson—to go on working and learning, to explore life by ourselves—she gave us a new strength." She had also taught us to make something of our life, to give our work its fullest meaning. Like Unamuno, she believed that those who have shared with others a common ideal, and fought together to make it a reality, have truly lived.

She, who had expressed in her poetry the need of breaking away from her own body, of dissolving into nature, had become all spirit, freed from any human limits. Her universe had been boundless; she had embraced all mankind in her Franciscan love of nature to form one vast country. From her childhood she had been interested in astronomy, in learning what existed beyond our world, which did not suffice for her. She had searched for God and the life beyond and she had met face to face with Him. Now she could move wherever her tired body had refused to take her and from where her destiny had carried her away—the Andes Mountains—among her beloved people of Monte Grande.

On Saturday, January 14, at ten o'clock, a Requiem Mass was celebrated for her by Cardinal Francis Spellman at St. Patrick's Cathedral. Her body was later taken to Bethpage Military Airport from where it was flown to Lima. A Chilean airplane waited there to bring her back to her own country on January 19.

President Carlos Ibáñez of Chile issued a statement saying: "Her death represents an irreparable loss of an exceptional soul for our country and for contemporary letters."[59] In deep grief, he decreed three days of national mourning. In all the schools and official buildings, the tricolor flag was flown at half-mast. A large escort walked beside the casket to the Casa Central of the University of Chile—state ministers, members of parliament and of the diplomatic corps, intellectuals, students, workers, people from all walks of life who had loved, admired, and respected her. The Rector of the University, Juan Gómez Millas, received her body in the Salón de Honor. Four hundred girls from Public High School No. 6 (whose first director Gabriela had been), formed a guard of honor and the choir of the University of Chile sang "Come, Sweet

Death" by Bach. More than two hundred thousand people paid their last respects to her.

On January 22, the funeral of Gabriela Mistral was held in the cemetery of Santiago where her body was temporarily placed in niche 97 of the mausoleum reserved for members of the Society of Primary Education, until it could be moved to Monte Grande. On the front of the granite monument was engraved a fragment of her poem "La oración de la maestra" (The Teacher's Prayer): "Lord, You who taught forgive me that I teach!" Within the niche were a frame with a parchment containing the complete poem "La oración" (The Prayer), and a bust of Gabriela, the work of Laura Rodig.

Tribute was paid to her in every Latin American country and in Europe. Israel, which does not give titles or medals to honor individuals, gave her name to a vast forest region containing thirty-five thousand trees. In Chile, a whole issue of the Annals of the University of Chile was dedicated to her. It consisted of articles and books written about her, as well as excerpts from some of her own works. An anthology was also published by Zig-Zag, in Santiago, in the year of her death. Commemorative stamps were issued in various countries. Her name had the same strength as the wind "maestral" or "mistral." Schools, libraries, centers bear her name. As far back as 1945, some schools had been named for her: two schools in Argentina, two in Chile, two in Colombia, three in Ecuador, one in Guatemala, two in Mexico, one in El Salvador. A public library was named for her in Vicuña, Chile, and one in Mexico, and busts and statues of her were erected in many countries. In October, 1959, in tribute to her, the Chilean painter Israel Roa exhibited his portraits of Gabriela Mistral at the University of Chile. Also in tribute and in accordance with her desire to encourage young writers, a literary contest for novels, essays, and poetry called "The Literary Contest Gabriela Mistral" was sponsored by the Municipality of Santiago.

It was not until 1960, three years after her death, that her final return to Monte Grande, the village of her happy childhood, took place under the auspices of the Ministry of the Interior. On March 22 and 23, at a deeply moving ceremony, tribute was rendered by the people of Chile to their spiritual mother. For that occasion, Doris Dana arrived in Santiago on March 11 as an official guest of the government. Dr. Tomás Tobar and Dr. Emilio Mohor had been called by the Legal Medical Institute to examine Gabriela's remains in case the body needed to be rearranged before the transfer took place. But upon opening the lid of the coffin, the two doctors were struck by the fact that Gabriela had not been touched by death. Dr. Mohor wrote of this striking experience:

"A soft serenity invaded that face that seemed to be touched by the hand of God.

"In three years and several months since her return from New York, death had not dared to touch her. Her eyelids remained closed, slightly of the color violet; her forehead, wide and clear; her finely chiseled nose.

"Her hands, white and regal, held a crucifix. Her black velvet dress which she had worn to receive the Nobel Prize for Literature from the hands of the King of Sweden, also remained intact. She still had the appearance of a queen."[60]

On March 22, at about 10:15, the casket was taken out of the niche by ten representatives of the Society of Writers of Chile and of the Society of Primary Education. Students from Public High School No. 6 of Santiago began to sing the "Ave María." Upon the coffin could be seen the habit of the Third Order of St.Francis in which Gabriela had wanted to be buried. A crown of red and white dahlias had been deposited the day before by the students of the school "Lucila Godoy." The ribbon attached to it bore the words "In reverence to the highest of teachers." The students from the Public High School Gabriela Mistral had placed a white fringe with the inscription "To our spiritual mother." Two bags containing the earth of Vicuña and Monte Grande lay near her. Ramón Luis Ortúzar, President of the Society of Primary Education, said in farewell: "Come back, then, beloved mortal remains, to the place of your forefathers and of your loves and smiles to form a tiny mount of silent earth under the shade of the guaiacum tree that softens the ardor of the rising sun. Beloved teacher and spiritual mother of the Chilean people, may your soul continue the fecund and noble life of immortality and glory."[61]

In the name of the city, the Mayor of Santiago, Ramón Alvarez Goldsack, paid the last tribute to Gabriela in the cemetery:

"The picture of her life was enveloped by the mystery of light and shade. She passed through prolonged periods of suffering, that sometimes were bitter, but she always kept her gentleness. One could apply to her the verse of Sophocles: 'I was born to give out love. not hatred.'

"She honored Chile as an exemplary teacher, because she left on the new generation, a moral imprint which illuminated her spirit as an educator."[62]

The apostolic administrator of Santiago, Monsignor Emilio Tagle Covarrubias, said a prayer for the repose of her soul and all those present recited the Lord's Prayer. Then the casket was placed in a military carriage pulled by six black horses and the official marchers followed on foot to the Plaza Ercilla. Behind the carriage were nine mounted spearmen, the civil and military authorities, and delegations of cadets from the Military School, the School of Carabineers and the Navy. Three girls from Public High No. 6 for Girls carried their school banner. The whole city of Santiago took part in this tribute and last farewell to Gabriela: the official members of the Government and of the Church, the various associations of writers and teachers, students, friends, and the people of Chile. In a circular, Luis Moll Briones, Director of Primary Education, had asked that all children in every school participate in a tribute to her:

"To render her homage as a humble teacher, pulled to the four cardinal points by her ardent love for children, manifested in her poetry as well as in her actions.

"Upon transferring her mortal remains to Monte Grande, in the Valley of Elqui, it is the wish of our Board of Primary Education that each student should learn to know and love the region that shaped Gabriela and will give her shelter. It is also our wish that the activities that commemorate this event should surpass any other customary cultural function so that they be the expression of a deep emotion."[63]

More than one thousand children from elementary and secondary schools stood on both sides of the streets as the carriage passed by, covering it with flowers. The schools honored her during the whole week, and, on the radio, programs about her life and work were given during the entire month of March. But perhaps the escort that had not been organized by anyone was the most moving; the simple people, laborers, workers, humble mothers in aprons, holding their babies in their arms, and barefoot children covered the coffin with a rain of petals.

At Plaza Ercilla, Gabriela's remains were transferred to Los Cerrillos Airport, from where they were flown to La Serena.

In the name of the city of La Serena, its Mayor, José Martínez Castillo, pronounced a eulogy:

"La Serena, next to her silence that flashes like a votive light, kneels with its hands joined together, as if imploring for her the peace and glory that in dismal days of hostility it was not capable of granting her. And it offers her as the highest gift the dazzled admiration of the provincial people, the suppressed tears of the Chilean children, the holy shadow of the redeeming cross and the prayers of its carnations. Take her, my friends, to the place where the Valley is born, near the solitary and bountiful vineyards, with that gentleness with which one carries a sleeping child, because the renowned Gabriela, crowned with stars, is the same Lucila who 'would speak to rivers, mountains, and reed fields.'"[64]

Then Monsignor Alfredo Cifuentes, Archbishop of La Serena, prayed for the repose of her soul.

On both sides of the road that led from La Serena to Vicuña could be seen lines of children from the secondary schools of La Serena as well as delegations of students from the Experimental Public High School Gabriela Mistral and the Public High School Diego Portales of Santiago. In the course of the sixty-five kilometers between La Serena and Vicuña, people of all walks of life had gathered along the road. When the funeral procession arrived in Vicuña, the birthplace of Gabriela, the people gathered in the main square, Plaza de Armas, in collective mourning. The Mayor, Guillermo Reyes, expressed their grief. Pedro Moral Quemado, a long-time friend of Gabriela and President of the Cultural Center Gabriela Mistral, spoke of her. Many years before, he had organized the Museum and Public Library Gabriela Mistral, which consists of some 4,380 books. Of these, 1,800 had been donated by Gabriela—all of them inscribed to her by their authors.

The journey continued to its final destination, Monte Grande, where the procession arrived at 4:50 P.M. There was an air of joy and sadness in the Valley of Elqui, of which Monte Grande is but a tiny portion. People had come from Coquimbo, Ovalle, La Serena, and other localities to receive Gabriela. Monte Grande, surrounded by green hills in the interior of the Province of Coquimbo, had found fame and recognition through her love. The humble village, which normally has no more than one thousand inhabitants, had on that memorable day more than five thousand people gathered to receive their own Gabriela. She, who had lived her childhood there and had dreamed of this earthly paradise, could at last rest in its hills.

The mausoleum, as she would have wanted it, is situated on the top of a small hill at the end of the village, not far from the church where she had received her First Communion. It consists of a vault opened in the earth itself with concrete walls. Upon it is erected a monolithic stone, work of the sculptor Felipe Núñez, according to the design of Luis Bertín. It bears the inscription: "Gabriela Mistral.—Premio Nobel 1945.—7-IV—1889—10-I—1957." Underneath is sculptured a laurel leaf and below that is recorded a thought written by Gabriela herself: "What the soul does for the body is what the artist does for his people. G.M." The mausoleum, which became a national monument, was erected by popular subscription under the auspices of the Society of Writers and the guidance of Julio Barrenechea and Carmen Castillo. The land on which it stands was a gift of two brothers, Guillermo and Juan Somerville Learmonth.

Upon her burial, Julio Barrenechea gave the following eulogy:

"You were the living statue of many things, our country's relic. You were the embodiment of the mother, of the suffering creator. You were the most perfected monument of the Chilean woman, from your humble pedestal to the heights of your glory.

"For all these reasons your homeland worships you, and is proud to be a country that knows how to pay tribute and which, upon looking at its reflection in the works of its artists, sees the image of a people with dignity.

"Gabriela Mistral, I would have liked to speak to you only with a long silence that resembles your serene majesty. Now, for your own peace, may the lights from the afternoon sky fade away and may you softly dream of your childhood as you lie under the small flowers that have come from all the corners of your valley." [65]

Emilio Pfeffer, the Under-Secretary of Education, evoked her majestic image:

"She has returned to become a part of the earth that was her cradle and that saw her swell with the passion for love and sacrifice. She comes followed by admiration and tears.

"We are here not to deliver her mortal remains to Monte Grande but to entrust the earth with the care and the adoration of beauty, the sharing with the best synthesis of humanity.

"May this place be the shrine from where the teacher irradiates her precepts full of feeling and tenderness that stem from the realm of the unknown, of which she gave us a glimpse with her great divinatory power."[66]

Luis Moll Briones, Director of Primary Education, wrote of her return to Monte Grande:

"A garden where there remained the echo of her laughter as a child and the memory of her cavalcades through the farmlands.

"Today the teacher returns to Monte Grande. The wishes of a lifetime have become fulfilled after her death.

"She returns to be closer to her school, to place her spirit within the reach of the delicate voices of her children.

"Thus, living again in spirit, she will go over the distant periods of her life when she was a rural schoolteacher, full of youth and hope.

"And her life, dedicated to culture, to schools, and to children, will pass once again, like a breath through the villages and cities of Chile, where she practiced her teaching, standing before the eager faces of the children of Los Andes, Antofagasta, Traiguén, Temuco, Punta Arenas, Santiago.

"Because Gabriela Mistral was above all a teacher; a teacher who understood the tragedy of poor children, the anguish of mothers; a teacher who, at the same time as she sought an effective method, probed into the depths of her inner self, reaching for the source of her poetry. Her best poems were dedicated to children but they were also an outlet for her deepest emotions as a woman."[67]

Gabriela now rests in peace among her people. To live on forever in Monte Grande had been her wish, not only because it was her real home, but because by her presence the needy children of the "tiny region of her childhood" would not be forgotten by others. She could help them even after her death. Warmer to her heart than all the official tributes she had received was the daily contact with young children who could now come to her, bringing on their donkeys simple flowers in a gesture of love.

On April 10, 1961, Doris Dana was sent by the State Department of the United States on a lecture tour in twelve Latin American countries to speak of her beloved friend Gabriela Mistral. She remained in Latin America, where she gave eighty-six lectures. She re-created through photographs, films, and tapes the familiar figure of Gabriela Mistral. Doris had brought records that introduced to the audience Gabriela's own voice, her conversations, her monologue about the poetry of Unamuno and Antero de Quental. In Chile, she distributed to the children a book by Gabriela Mistral called *Poesías completas*, (Complete Works of Poetry), which had been published in Spain in 1958 by Aguilar. In Gabriela's name she gave out books and warm clothing in different parts of Chile.

I, who knew her, still see her as vividly as during her life: tall, majestic, humble with the poor and proud with the rich, dressed with the austere simplicity of a prophet, embellishing everything that she touched. This outstanding woman had transcended her own sufferings and her personal needs, and had embraced within her ample reach all of God's creatures—men and women, children, animals—and the very elements of nature. She, who had no children of her own, became the mother of all abandoned children, the sister of ill-treated women and of abused laborers, the defender of peace and justice. Her poetry is universal, the children that she lulled to sleep are those of any country of the entire world. Yet, it was in Chile that she first came in contact with God and His creation. It was in the country of her childhood that her feeling of union with the elements was nurtured and came to encompass the sea, the mountains, the trees of the whole universe.

Gabriela had traveled all her life. At times she felt exiled from her country and her people and out of touch with them. Because she lived for such long periods in non-Spanish-speaking countries she was perhaps more conscious of her native roots. For the same reason, she wanted to keep alive the oral forms of her language. She thus watched over it as over a living being so that it would not be exiled and replaced by the language of the country she lived in. She would always reminisce with nostalgia on the various regions of Chile. Salvador de Madariaga, the Spanish philosopher, who also had led a nomadic life and could understand Gabriela's reactions, said of her: "Universal in spirit, wanderer through continents, Gabriela Mistral lived and died with her heart in Chile." [68]

There is no better expression of her constant love for Chile and for children than her posthumous work *Poema de Chile* written during her last journey through life, far away from her native land. In this poem, she expresses her longing for the country she knew as a child and as a young woman, and it is there that she wishes to return after her death. Gabriela the spirit and Lucila the child she once was come together when the poet and the little Indian boy join hands to walk over their land with a reverence for life. The magic of this poem is that it unites the world of fantasy and the world of reality; it draws a perfect circle around her previous works to bind them together: the delicate dream world of childhood found in *Ternura* and a detachment from her physical self in a sublime love for others, as expressed in *Lagar*. The circle, a geometrical figure that has no beginning and no end, represents eternity and perfection in a supreme God, the author of all Creation. Gabriela leaves her little friends, just as she had come to them in simplicity and love, to rejoin that Supreme Being in Heaven: "I now hear the call of Him who is my Master." [69]

CHAPTER 4

Gabriela Mistral's Religious Concept

> *"Many years from now, when I shall be but a tiny silent mount of dust, play with me, my children, play with the earth my bones will have become."*
>
> GABRIELA MISTRAL

Gabriela Mistral was a woman of action whose feet were deeply-rooted in the reality of her American Continent. She was concerned with the physical well-being of the common people whom she always called the "beautiful people." But she was also a woman of meditation who lifted her eyes to God and brought Him down to earth so that people would see in Him the familiar face of a friend. She was equally concerned with their spiritual well-being. Religion was not confined to the Church or to the Temple, but was to be an integral part of daily life, a constant companion to social progress: "I am not one of those who believe that love is the only great event in life; I believe that it is just as important to open our consciousness to the awareness of both the supernatural world and the world of social problems and it seems to me that the fulfillment of a work of art is a solemn event."[1]

The French writer Max Daireaux said of her personal form of religion: "She is a Christian, not according to the Church but according to Christ; her mysticism is, as it were, the poetry of suffering."[2]

Gabriela was born and died a Catholic, but her Catholicism was truly contemporary and might be called basic Christianity. She felt a close kinship with the prophets of the Old and the New Testaments. Her God was the God of the Jews and her Savior was Jesus Christ, God made Man. Christianity also meant for her

119

the gentle tenderness of the Child Jesus and His Mother, the Virgin Mary. She had a new and dynamic conception, later to be preached in the Ecumenical Council by Pope John XXIII and Paul VI. It was a complete return to the Bible and the preaching of the first Christians, a religion rooted in poverty and simplicity and motivated by a strong social sense.

For a time, in the early part of the 1910's, she moved away from the Catholic faith and sought an answer in Theosophy, which attracted many intellectuals in Europe and America. She became interested in Oriental philosophy and literature. She saw in Buddhism high mystic principles: to accept suffering as a form of life, to reach a state of *nirvana,* or supreme annihilation of self: ". . . Theosophy, then Buddhism, gave me the experience of the heroic and supernatural in my youth; when I was twenty, these doctrines were for me my Tannhäuser or my Parsifal."[3] The concept of reincarnation also attracted her because it stressed the sacredness of life.

On one occasion, Gabriela called Asia "Mother" in order to express her belief that the Indians of Latin America had originally come from there and had been followers of Buddha: ". . . through Rabindranath Tagore I have been made to recall a certain form of religious popular song that one of my ancestors sang in front of Buddha, with a fixed gaze. Many so-called imitations are but a rediscovering and a finding of that which is ours and was lost somewhere along the road."[4]

In the early 1920's, after a deep inner search, Gabriela came back to a strengthened Catholicism and told a friend that she had become a member of the Third Order of St. Francis. She revealed, through the many articles that she wrote, her firm belief in Christianity and her special kinship with past and present spiritual leaders. She felt that from an Oriental mystic she had again become a Catholic. More precisely she perhaps meant that Oriental philosophy had for a short time served as an outlet for her mystic need of God, but that she had found a deeper, more meaningful, and merciful truth in Christianity. She said to a friend in 1925:

"I was a mystic. I am now a Catholic and, furthermore, I belong to the Third Order of St. Francis. It is an Order for lay people. I have of course certain obligations. For example, I must give at least ten per cent of everything I earn. . . . The peasants in

Spain are such devout Catholics. The people there are extra-ordinary. Saintliness is not unusual . . . They have left their mark on me."[5]

In 1926, in an article about Romain Rolland, whom she greatly admired for his spiritual personality, she professed her Catholicism. Rolland who was attracted to Buddhism and had not as yet returned to Catholicism could not understand her faith:

"He called my faith, if my memory does not fail me, an idea that had been worn by time, wasted away and dead. And he reproached me, with the kindest reproach, for my return to it. Why does this great master whom I worship and whose opinion, for this very reason, deeply affects me, refuse to understand that I have once again embraced the living flame of the Catholic faith? I have come to warm myself in the hearth of my Spanish mystics. . . ."[6]

Each of her books marked an evolution in her faith; from a faltering search for God she came to a firm belief in eternal life. In a commentary on poems of Rabindranath Tagore, first published in 1917, she yearned to see God, awaiting Him in a way similar to that of the bride in the Song of Songs, but she still expressed doubt about her ability to come face to face with Him. She had experienced religious fervor, but not as yet a mystic encounter with Him:

". . . I spoke to them of You, without yet having known You. You will forgive me my Lord, won't You? It was their yearning, and it was also my longing to see you as clearly as the leaves of a lily.

". . . Yes, it is the same as when we await with expectant eyes, watching over the road. The one we are waiting for does not come, but the burning fire in our eyes draws at every moment an outline of his face on the pale horizon."[7]

Gabriela felt a thirst to possess and be possessed by God: "I have struggled a great deal. People are mistaken when they believe that I am gentle and tranquil. They say that my face is serene, but my heart is on fire. This heart has made me search for God through many ardent brambles."[8] Her love of God was as natural to her as breathing; in her religious fervor she conversed with Him as with a close and personal friend and she meditated for hours upon the mysteries of life and death. She felt that man is united to Christ from the moment he is born until he dies:

We cling to you, as the child to his mother,
from our first cry to our last agony. [9]

Gabriela understood that to reach God one should have a complete experience of life, should know the depths of suffering and joy. The greatest joy is to be able to help others; only those who can do something for others have the right to live: "There is the joy of being healthy and the joy of being just; but above all there is the infinite joy of being useful to others." [10] She also said: "Only those who live for an ideal, or who live for their fellow men, deserve to live." [11] She came to love Sister Juana Inés de la Cruz, the Mexican nun and writer who embodied Christian humility, renouncing knowledge and the worldly court to care for the sick, for the daily chores of the convent: "And she looks for even more suffering; she longs for the lash of discipline, she feels the bitterness of blood on her chastised waist. This is for me the most beautiful moment in her life; without this hour I would not love her." [12]

Gabriela felt that innocence and simplicity are the way to God, the two fundamental qualities needed to reach perfection in God and in one's own work. She, therefore, loved and protected children and all those who were like children. She was deeply influenced by Jesus' love for children and those who retained a youthful spirit. Children were to her the embodiment of the Christ-Child and, therefore, the symbol of Christianity. They will be the way to Christ, "such a long road to Christ, that it has encircled the earth." [13] For this reason, she felt a special closeness for St. Vincent de Paul because he showed the importance of charity and embraced the cause of abandoned children:

"At sixty he has become the great protector of abandoned children, those small ones who are nameless. They are the true children of God and could well bear the name of Jesus Christ. . . . In this endeavor his life wears away; with the perfume of babes in arms, with the moist hair of the five month old, and with the gesture of a tiny hand reflected in his melancholy eyes that were mentioned by his biographer. His days are coming to an end and time, the patron of mankind, takes leave of him." [14]

She also admired St. Theresa of the Child Jesus, the young French saint, because her way to God was through "the narrow path of spiritual childhood."[15] She felt that divine grace could only be found in those who knew not that they possessed it, in the limpid eyes of a child, in the humble gesture of a simple woman:

Divine Grace is such a delicate thing,
so gentle and silent that those who possess it
can never speak of it,
that they carry it in their voice and in their gestures
or that it dwells indefinable
in the air, in a voice, in a gaze.
I never reached it, my little one,
but I caught a glimpse of it
in the eyes of a child
and of an old man
and in a woman bent over her work
or in the beckoning call of a mountain. [16]

Her dynamic conception of Christianity was focused on youth and she saw in every religious act the participation of the Creator and His creation:

"If there ever was a religious act it is this: Religious is everything that implies an action that leaps over the present like an arrow toward a far away future. Religious is the act of faith which calls upon the forces of life, because this call is an invocation of the divine. We plant a small root down deep in the ground and we conjure the invisible energy of water, of the air, and of light, so that they may cooperate. It is a prayer to God the Creator, who continues the humble act that we began."[17]

1. *Social Awareness and Justice*

Gabriela wanted above all to impart to others a religious spirit that would be mingled with a sense of social justice. She felt that it was time to reevaluate one's belief in order to achieve a spiritual awakening: "It is the hour of awakening that summons all the religious consciences of our planet and exhorts them to re-examine the natural and supernatural life of the Blessed Lord that we willingly adopted as the norm of our life and our death."[18] As a confirmed Catholic who had known years of search and self-analysis, she felt compelled to examine the reasons for the growing materialism in the world, and to help lessen it. As long as there is materialism, Christ will remain nailed to the Cross:

> *I look at you, body of my Christ,*
> *hanging from the cross*
> *still crucified.*
> *I shall sing when*
> *your nails have been unfastened!*
> *When shall it be? When?*
> *I have been waiting at your feet*
> *for two thousand years,*
> *and as I wait, my tears flow.*[19]

Christianity, she would say, is not only a sublime soliloquy with God but a divine and dynamic power to be used against the forces of materialism. It is not only the recitation of passages of the Bible or of the catechism but a living element that directs the life of people and of nations. The complete meaning of Christianity is perfection: "Christendom is not moved by half measures. It finds inner peace only when it sees, touches, and breathes perfection. We are striving toward it and we will reach it."[20] Christianity is a doctrine of equality that should reach the poor as well as the rich.

She realized as early as 1924 that a fundamental element of Christianity was missing in the daily practice of religion: social awareness and social justice. She wanted to see the union of social classes, as was preached in the Gospels. Christ brought both an individual and a collective message to men. This message should be given to all. For a few it provides the means for reaching the highest mystical state; for most people it provides rules for daily life: "If we are total Christians of the total Gospel, we will go to the people. We shall organize a little the confused yearnings for reforms within our economic system and, together, we will first discuss and then we shall grant."[21] The social aspect in religion was of great importance to her. In a conversation with the philosopher Giovanni Papini she said: "I think, I would even venture to affirm, that poverty is not an enemy of spiritual progress, but misery is. With the exception of superior beings, misery defaces life and hardens the soul. For me, half of religion is charity that searches, that bears upon the earth with bleeding feet."[22]

Gabriela wanted the Church to remember daily its democratic

origin; she wanted to see a new youth who would be proud to express its faith and that, some day, would be capable of setting up reforms. Christ had not come to earth for a selected few but as the Savior of humanity. She strongly believed that He had a fundamental place in all schools, for He was a liberator and discoverer, He was "The Most Perfect One" who had come to the world with the highest form of beauty:

"But I want to speak about the right of Jesus to be in the public school. Is there not a place for him on the walls covered with liberators, discoverers, and wise men? He was a liberator; he freed the ancient world from abjectness and from the cruelty of a cult in which blood was spilled. He was a discoverer, he brought light to entire spiritual continents. One critic, who was an unbeliever, wrote that Jesus added to the best of ancient philosophies something noble and unknown until then. He revealed the only science that blossoms into happiness and which brings harmony amongst men. He destroyed in the Roman Empire the insolent excess of luxury and the vice that blurs the clear human faculties; he wiped out the imperial tyranny that forbade Christians to love a higher God and obliged them to worship impure deities. He destroyed many other things, but these are enough. And the Most Perfect One even left us a new literature in his parables and in his Sermon on the Mount. A nectar of an unsavored higher beauty is diffused in his writings, and it is not possible to find in Roman literature a single page that is equal to his words as spoken by St. Mark or St. Matthew."[23]

In an autobiographical note that she wrote in her early years she explained her credo: "I am a Christian, a complete advocate of democracy. I believe that Christianity, with deep social awareness, can save nations."[24]

2. *Religious Unity and Tolerance*

Gabriela had a vision of religion that was far in advance of her time. She recognized religious freedom for all faiths—Judaism, Catholicism, Protestantism, and others—but she felt a thirst for religious unity. She did not accept the schism as something permanent; she believed in a possible reconciliation between the Christian faiths and in an understanding of the Jews: "And whenever I see that a man or a woman considers the Christian schism as an irremediable fact, buried and forgotten, I feel a strange repulsion. Because the vastness of the sea terrifies me, it is like hell itself.''[25] She felt that men ought to live as brothers, for when they fight each other for religious reasons they are crucifying Christ a second time. As early as 1925 she wrote that Catholics and Protestants should unite in order to fight against materialism. In their struggle against one another they only weaken the power of the spirit and increase the number of atheists: ''Sooner or later, at a time of distress, the two branches of the Christian faith will realize that this struggle between them is the greatest misfortune for the moral future of the people. . . . Our task is to bring the young people to Christ.''[26]

At various times between 1924 and 1949 Gabriela wrote for *Nueva Democracia,* a religious magazine which firmly believed in a closer understanding of various faiths. She admired in Protestants their social awareness and their constant contact with the Bible. While visiting a North American school in the South of Chile, she expressed her gratitude and emotion when she was asked to read a passage of the Bible to the Protestant children. She chose one of the Psalms of David.

She felt that every man should know and respect every other man's religion because religion is not only a belief but also an expression of a people's culture: ''Not only should religions be tolerated within a nation, but they must be invited to work actively in the shaping of the people.''[27] A Jewish girl, who was a student of hers, wanted to be excused from a course on religion. Gabriela asked her to stay in the class for a month, not to convert her, but to acquaint her with Christianity, which is not only found in liturgy but in every form of life, in every work of art: ''She remained not only a month, but a year. She was not converted, of course, nor did I, who know the Jewish people, expect it of her; but I know that during that class hour she enjoyed this life-giving confrontation and it was for her the most enriching hour of all.''[28]

As early as 1935 Gabriela defended the cause of the Jewish people and praised their intelligence and ability, which she called the Jewish genius. However, she felt that the modern Jew, like the Christian, had lost his faith and that present-day materialism had changed his natural religious temperament. She believed that Christianity owed a great deal to Judaism, for mysticism which is such an important part of Christianity is based on its Hebraic beginnings. She felt responsible for the suffering of the Jewish people at the outbreak of the Second World War and asked Latin America to receive them in a humanitarian and Christian way:

"Of all human metals there is none more sorely tried by tongues of fire and hammering in a world made full of suffering. There is no web of flesh more pricked and cut by needle and spear. And it is a suffering of a special kind, a terrible kind of pain invented for him rather than for the Chinese or the Zulu: suffering through humiliation, scorn, and loathing."[29]

In 1948 she hoped to see Latin America free of xenophobia so that immigrants from other nations could find a new home there: "I feel it is a tragic proof of stupidity to see a human being hating or belittling his fellow man because of his skin or the color of his eyes, his height or his language."[30]

Gabriela recalled the massive wind-beaten cross of the Christ of the Andes as a symbol of peace between Argentina and Chile. Peace was to her the most important word in the Gospels and she hoped that every man, no matter what his faith, would remember it and utter it every day. To love peace is to love God and obey Him. It is also to love children:

"To love peace is simply to love life and to love the world like a cluster of all nations we have not yet seen, but will come to know. And to maintain peace is simply to obey the Creator who wishes no harm or dishonor to be brought on His creation: man and nature. To ask for peace is the same as asking for elemental nourishment such as milk or bread. . . .

"It is necessary to love peace until we are filled with it and care for it as much as we care for the receptacle of our blood, which we call body. It is necessary to know that peace becomes fused with the love of God and it is His law."[31]

3. *Feeling for the Bible*

Gabriela did not arrive at religion through the power of reason but through the impulses of the heart and an intense need for God. Actually, she could not understand theologians who analyzed the Bible, for true knowledge comes from within. To her, the Bible, both the Old and the New Testaments, was the most important book in the world and an indispensable companion. It was the one book without which man cannot live; it represented to her strength and tenderness:

"The Bible is the only book for me. I cannot understand how anyone who lives without it would not be impoverished, nor how anyone could be strong without its substance, nor gentle without its softness." [32]

"We all have our own concept of the Bible and we extract from this mighty book what corresponds to our particular mood; the expression 'biblical education' does not mean anything concrete, because some absorb the dry, invigorating tonic of Solomon; others have their intense and substantial relaxed moments with Isaiah, and the one hundred per cent puritan seems to fix his preference on the writings of Moses." [33]

> Oh Bible, my noble Bible, extraordinary panorama
> upon which my eyes have set,
> you keep within the Psalms a burning lava
> and I kindle my heart in their rivers of fire!
>
> You sustained my people with your hearty wine
> and you raised them to their feet,
> strong and erect, in the midst of men.
> My heart leaps with joy when I utter your name;
> for I come from you and I have overcome destiny. [34]

Gabriela used to read the Bible over and over and underline in different colored pencils the passages that answered her current needs. She made many annotations in her copy of Cipriano de Valera's translation of the Bible, which she donated to the library of Public High School No. 6 for Girls of Santiago. In the blank pages that precede Genesis she wrote in blue pencil one of her most beautiful poetic prose pieces dedicated to the Bible, dated 1919. It revealed her personal and intimate feeling for the Bible and her oneness with its prophets. Here is part of what she wrote:

"My book, book of mine, at any season and at any time, a good friend for my soul, strong and powerful companion. You have taught me in brief songs the noble beauty and the simple candor, the simple and frightening truth. My best friends have not been people of my time, but those that you gave me: David, Ruth,

Job, Rachel, and Mary. . . . Braving the passing of time, you have come to me, and I have dissolved centuries into nothingness to meet with you, I walk amidst you, I am one of yours like one of those who worked, suffered and lived in your time and within the reach of your light.

"How many times have you comforted me? As many times as my face was pressed against the earth. Have I rushed to you in vain, oh book of mankind, the only book? Through David, I learned to love songs, songs that gently rock human bitterness. Ecclesiastes gave rise to that old sigh of mine when confronted with the futility of life, and your intonation has become so much mine that I no longer know whether I tell my lament or whether I am only repeating that of your men of suffering and repentance. I have never tired of you, the way one grows tired of poems written by men. You are always soothing, newly discovered, like the grass in July and your sincerity is the only one in which I can never find a flaw, a hidden nest of lies. Your nakedness frightens the hypocrite, and your purity is hateful to the libertine, and I love you in your entirety, from the fragrance of the parables to the harsh words of Numbers."[35]

Gabriela felt that nothing could be strong enough to take the power and the radiance of the Bible away. Its beauty had been revealed to her by intuition and not by intellectual knowledge:

"Scholars pull you apart with their clumsy instruments of logic to reject you, I have sat down to love you for ever and to nourish my heart with your voice during all the days that my Master allows me to look at His light. Teachers fill with subtle explanations the margin of your pages; they modify and classify, but I love you. . . .

"Oh Bible, cradle song of all people, eternal mother who nourishes us, you are filled with purity and knowledge, I need you for ever. Do not leave me. I shall always be enough of a child so that your unaffected simplicity will never surprise me. You shall always satiate me, filling my cup which longs for God."[36]

Gabriela marked some of her favorite passages in that copy of the Bible. Some of them are noted here. Genesis, Chapter 24, Verses 3 to 67, and Chapter 30, Verse 1: "And when Rachel saw that she bare Jacob no children, Rachel envied her sister; and said unto Jacob, give me children, or else I die."[37] Book of

Job, Chapter 5, Verses 23 to 26:

"For thou shalt be in league with the stones of the field: and the beasts of the field shall be at peace with thee.

"And thou shalt know that thy tabernacle shall be in peace; and thou shalt visit thy habitation, and shalt not sin.

"Thou shalt know that thy seed shall be great, and thine offspring as the grass of the earth.

"Thou shalt come to thy grave in a full age, like as a shock of corn cometh in his season."[38]

The Song of Solomon, Chapter 5, Part IV, Verse 2, and Part V, Verse 6: "I sleep, but my heart waketh: it is the voice of my beloved that knocketh, saying, Open to me, my sister, my love, my dove, my undefiled: for my head is filled with dew, and my locks with the drops of the night."[39] "I opened to my beloved; but my beloved had withdrawn himself, and was gone: my soul failed when he spoke: I sought him, but I could not find him; I called him, but he gave me no answer."[40] The Book of Psalms was marked in several places. In the New Testament, among other passages, she underlined St. Luke, Chapter 11, Verses 9 and 10: "And I say unto you, Ask and it shall be given you; seek, and ye shall find; knock, and it shall be opened unto you. For every one that asketh receiveth; and he that seeketh findeth; and to him that knocketh it shall be opened."[41] St. Matthew, the Sermon on the Mount, Chapter 5, Verse 13: "Ye are the salt of the earth: but if the salt have lost his savour, wherewith shall it be salted? It is thenceforth good for nothing, but to be cast out, and to be trodden under foot of men."[42]

4. *Contemplation of God's Creation*

Gabriela was very much influenced by Genesis. She knew that God had created the universe for the enjoyment of men, but that they took it for granted and mistreated it. Men delighted in the things that God had created for them, but they never saw Him in these things. Yet beauty in the universe was the shadow of God. Gabriela praised God's creation and in so doing she praised Him. She felt united with His creation and, therefore, with Him, and her mysticism was thus similar to that of St. Francis:

I believe in my heart that asks
for nothing because it is capable of the highest of
  dreams
and it embraces in that dream all of creation:
What an infinite master![43]

Gabriela wrote about God's wrath at men's insensitiveness. In a parable, first published in 1913 under the title "La defensa de la belleza" (In Defense of Beauty) and later as "Por qué las rosas tienen espinas" (Why Roses have Thorns), she explained the meaning of thorns on roses. Even though God had wanted beauty to be kind and accessible to men, when He heard roses complain of men's cruelty, He felt obliged to create thorns in order to protect them from such mistreatment. She believed that men ought to take time to contemplate God's creation. In another parable, "La Pascua de los pájaros" (The·Birds Christmas), published in *Sucesos,* December, 1915, Gabriela showed the Master as He went to the forest to leave locks of His hair on trees so that the birds might build their. nests. In the meantime, "Noel" (Santa Claus) brought gifts to the children in the cities. In still another ,parable, "Proyectos" (Projects), published in Manuel Guzmán Maturana's *Segundo Libro de Lectura* (Second Book of Reading Selections) in 1916-1917, she told of the different goals of three grandsons: to follow the sea, to work on the land, to contemplate God's creation: "There is also holiness in being a lover of God's work, to feel it in depth and gather it in reverence. I shall not do any other thing as long as my eyes are open to this profound and delicate wonder."[44] In another story, Gabriela wrote that Our Lord had two footstools: one was the earth, the other the hearts of men, and God rested His feet on both. But when men became independent and knew sensuality and hatred, the footstool broke. God kept His foot upon the earth, which had accepted His dominion: "This is why the earth blossoms in springtime and the snow scorched by the sun melts and flows. The little bugs swarm among the bushes."[45]

The following ten commandments of the gardener published in *Sucesos* in 1913 express the thought that men ought to contemplate the universe and care for its flowers so as to maintain the beauty handed to them by God:

"1. To give back to the earth its primitive beauty, for God

handed it down to man full of flowers and he, in turn, debased it day after day;

"2. To place in the retina of the eyes and the soul beautiful visions, for sepultures give gloomy thoughts, flowers offer thoughts of love;

"3. So that the dew from heaven may have divine cups on which to alight and be retained for a time, instead of falling and losing itself into the unclean earth;

"4. So that the bright colored butterflies may have a fragrant petal that rocks them to and fro; so that the golden bees may prepare the special nectar of the gods;

"5. So that the temple of the Lord and the house of man may be adorned with something more delicate than coldly wrought metal and lifeless timber;

"6. So that the wind may free itself of the exhalation of the polluted breath of men, beasts, and disintegrated matter;

"7. So that the bird may have its fair share in total grace and harmony;

"8. So that women who are too poor to buy for themselves pearls, rubies, and amethysts, may find in the rose, the jasmine, and the violet, pearls, rubies, and amethysts to adorn their brow, their breast, and their hands;

"9. So that the poor suffering human being that man is may possess new generous resources to heal the leprosy of his flesh and of his spirit;

"10. So that they may remain in their place to proclaim the cult of its Royal Highness, the Ideal, now that the age of machine and of the dollar threatens to break the neck of the sacred swan."[46]

5. *Beauty and Perfection in One's Work*

For Gabriela as for Jacques Maritain, her spiritual brother, to develop a love for beauty was a way of coming closer to God and to perfection. Gabriela sought the essence of things and saw beauty in an act of humility, in an intense expression of spiritual anguish, in the root of a plant. In many instances she expressed what beauty meant to her and how essential it is to discover it: "I have always admired the capacity to admire, which is for me an unmistakable sign of a noble people, of a bright spiritual life and of a truthful blood."[47] She said:

"I love beauty and I kneel beside it wherever it may be."[48] "And beauty is for me like a powerful wind that runs freely over the world, refreshing the burning cheeks of the gleaners, beating against the light clothes of children as they weave a circle on the plain holding each others' hands. The wind enters people's houses in a big wave of good health."[49]

In her search for beauty and perfection, Gabriela felt a kinship with artists of the Middle Ages, and Renaissance for their work was filled with God's message. She praised the works of such early artists as Donatello, Giotto, Simone di Martini, and Fra Angelico. She also greatly admired Michelangelo, the overpowering figure of the Italian Renaissance. These sculptors and painters were greatly inspired by the Old and the New Testaments; in the Old Testament they were drawn to the strength and energy of prophets such as Elijah, Moses, David; in the New Testament to the gentleness of Jesus, his Mother, and the disciples. Gabriela wrote of Donatello and his masterpiece, St. John:

"I find the statue of St. John in a side chapel, well protected by strong bronze gratings. I approach it, filled with reverence: I love Donatello, the man with supernatural hands whose life has lifted my soul so many times; and I also love the man who was the first to baptize men. . . .Passion twists his body from the tendons of his neck to the nerves of his feet, oh those feet that walked a hundred roads."[50]

She received from the paintings by Fra Angelico his message of religious ecstasy:

"No one before the Blessed One had ever depicted ecstasy; it was like giving substance to the vibrations of the atmosphere; this was the message he brought. He lived in daily rapture; what was for others an event that happens once in a lifetime, was for him as familiar as the beads on his Dominican rosary. He let adoration pour forth from his heart and he placed it in his frescoes."[51]

She was drawn to Michelangelo's statue of the adolescent David, calling him her "lover"; but King David of the Psalms was to her "Father David." Gabriela felt a deep serenity while looking at Michelangelo's statue of Moses, similar to her feeling when she read Dante and the Book of Job. She made a distinction between

Moses and the Christian saints. She was deeply moved by the spiritual rhythm that arose from the statue:

"He is surrounded by an aura, not the Christian halo that vibrates around his head, but the so-called vital aura that shines as powerful around the feet and the flanks as well as the forehead and we receive that light upon ourselves. It is like a bubbling spring with great rhythms that comes forth from the depths of his heart. We become part of this rhythm; the tyranny of the sublime takes hold of our blood, and we no longer know when we are 'in tune' and we have lost our own pulsation."[52]

In the same way, she admired Jean-Baptiste Marie Vianney, the French saint who brought to the nineteenth century a new religious fervor, reminiscent of the Middle Ages: "His arms were created to lift up the Sacred Host, and for no other weight than this holy gesture of Elevation. . . . The simplicity found in a machine or in architecture was what gave his speech the power of conviction which fell like lead from his pulpit to his listeners."[53]

Because she particularly understood the religious art of the Middle Ages when artists had respect for their work, she deplored the uniformity of modern religious art. An artisan of the Middle Ages or of the Renaissance would create an original work, but in modern times, Gabriela said, ten thousand statues made of plaster and garishly colored come from one mold: "The twelfth, thirteenth, and fourteenth centuries understood their saints, as men who suffer and are passionate. These saints had a heart that knew the highest of pressures, they were like divine lions. . ."[54]

Gabriela felt that the soul should be part of whatever a man does. Mysticism means not only union with God but also union with one's work:

"This is called the thrust of a vocation and one becomes marked by it for ever, . . . Bernard Palissy had his own concept of mysticism wrapped up in the sand and in the clay of his art, and he said that God had made him understand—what he meant was that God had called him to other rough and hidden paths, to the magnificent field of craftsmanship."[55]

Work was like a pressure of the spirit on the palms of the hands; thus, it was important to select one's vocation in harmony with one's talent and soul:

"But the soul, I answered him, cannot be turned off like water, nor can it be dismissed from our work like a cumbersome mother-in-law. Only because the soul is interwoven with everything we do—whether it be beautiful or ugly—our work is an important matter . . . the soul seems like a partner and passion is so visible that it can almost be touched." [56]

"Then one makes a selection, and it has to be made with a sharp eye and after careful pondering, as if one was choosing a wife, for one's work lasts longer than a woman and as long as children. Let us choose our profession with a sincere confession of what we are, of what our arms are capable of doing, what our soul is most fond of, what we can accomplish with enthusiasm and not with bitterness. . . . It is a religious act, the most religious of all acts, to choose the workshop of an electrician, or the school for horticulture, to become part of a trade." [57]

> *Children, to you I say,*
> *every trade is blessed,*
> *to dig the ground, to knead the bread,*
> *to kiss with passionate lips the holy cilice;*
> *all are worthy paths, all are sweet exercises*
> *through which men set out on their way to God.* [58]

Because of her deeply religious attitude toward work, Gabriela demanded much of herself both as a writer and a teacher. She once wrote: "Hasten to leave an imprint of your soul upon your work." [59] She did not feel worthy to bear the name of "teacher" that Jesus Christ bore. She looked upon him as a supreme example and "Friend" and asked him to help her reach spiritual fulfillment in her love of children. Her poem "La maestra rural" (The Rural Schoolteacher), of which she said: "There goes the only poem of which I am fond. . . . I do not like it for its artistic quality, but for its religious concept," [60] expresses Gabriela's religious intensity:

> *Her soul was like an overflowing vase*
> *that poured forth dew drops upon the human race;*
> *and her life was a wide breach*
> *that Our Lord opens to thrust his light.* [61]

Gabriela also wrote a prayer for students so that they would start each new day with the Grace of God upon them. Here are some of her thoughts:

"I invoke you, my Lord, Master of divine grace, as I begin my day's work. May your divine grace enter my closed door and place its hand upon me. Without you, my studies would be worthless, and I do not want my work to be with lamentation.

". . . May you enlighten the gropings of my mind, like a white flash of lightning. May you give it the capacity for discerning sharp fragrances so that it may convey that which is unutterable.

". . . May you walk into my mind like children walk over the earth.

". . . May your divine grace grant me the vision of images of fire known to John and the simple words of Peter, the fisherman.

"At your touch, may enthusiasm melt the ice from my heart, and my blood flow faster in my work and my eyes shine brighter with an inner fire.

"Through your divine grace, may my thoughts have instead of the rigid order of words the spontaneous disorder of living herbs.

"May you descend upon me in my dreams as well as in my vigil, so that I may awake each day enriched and the miracle of dawn be like the discovery of a nest of turtledoves in the wheat...

". . . Oh Master of divine grace, I ask of you to bestow upon me this divine gift as I begin my daily work. Your names are many, but I choose to call you by this name. Pierce me with your divine grace. Your arrow is swift, but does not spill blood; it sets us aflame."[62]

In a similar way, Gabriela wrote the ten commandments of the artist, of which a few are mentioned here:

"I. You shall love beauty which is the shadow of God upon the universe.

"III. You shall not use beauty to lure the senses but as the natural nourishment of the soul.

"VII. Your beauty shall also receive the name of compassion and you shall console the hearts of men.

"X. From all your creative work you shall emerge with a sense of shame because it was inferior to your dream and inferior to that most marvelous dream of God which is nature."[63]

6. *The Power of Prayer*

An important element of solace for Gabriela was the confidence that she placed in prayer. She firmly believed in the power of prayer, even the prayers of people who did not have a strong conviction, or, the prayers of those who belonged to different denominations. After the death of her nephew, she yearned for the moment that they would meet again. She had attained certainty concerning eternal life. Her attitude was no longer combative, she was drawing closer to God and becoming detached from the world: "I live more than ever with the certainty of an eternal life and there is only one thought that appeases me and that rocks me to sleep each night: no longer will I have to leave him and live my after life alone. I will soon experience my after life with him."[64]

Gabriela herself prayed fervently for the living and for the dead. Her prayers were not only traditional prayers learned by heart but spontaneous dialogues between her soul and God. In her youth she had rebelled, even argued with God, and she thus established with Him a personal and direct contact. Unlike the Spanish mystics who began their union with Him in contemplation and serenity, she had her beginnings in anguish and torment. A mystic was to her ". . . one who has a twofold vision and a multiplied strength."[65] "The mystic is always half passion and half confusion; he is a man who enters a burning cloud that sweeps him away into ecstasy. . . . The mystic believes that intuition is the only window open to truth and he closes his eyes, looking down on intellect, for the world of form is the world of appearances."[66] Her prayers always came from within. They sought God in simplicity and expressed an awareness of her fellow creatures:

"Our Lord's prayer begins and ends in a peremptory and inevitable plural, similar to the blows of a hammer and to the thrusts of litanies. The prayers that came later are for the most part of a personal nature and perhaps for this reason they are counterprayers, a malignant return to ourselves. We suffered a fall when we forgot the "us" in our prayers as if our conscience had become hollow and lethargic. The act of praying became mechanical and the essence of prayer a simple discovery."[67]

She believed in the unifying power of prayer and she found in it protection for those she loved and strength. When she prayed for the safety of her Brazilian war protégé José Rumayor Netto, she wrote: "We are also happy that you ask those who are close to you to pray for you. We say special prayers for the Allied cause and for you, at your mother's house and àt mine. This assistance will not fail you, it is more sustaining than all the help that you, soldiers with helmets and boots, seek and long for."[68] She also prayed for the souls of friends who had commited suicide. She could never condemn a man who in a moment's loss of grace had put an end to his days.

Gabriela had learned her first prayers from her mother, and her first knowledge of the Bible, in particular the Old Testament, had come from her paternal grandmother:

"Now that the child puts words together like small pieces of stained glass, you place upon his lips a slight prayer and there it remains, alive until the last day of his life. This creation is as simple as the stalk of the lily and it reaches, tremulous, toward our Lord's eyes. With this brief prayer we ask for everything that is needed to lead a gentle and pure life on the tormented crust of the earth; we ask for our daily bread, we repeat that all men are our brothers and we praise the mighty will of God."[69]

"I do not recall when I heard for the first time the words of the Bible. As a little girl I heard the stories of the Bible from my sister Emelina and, before that, from my grandmother, on my father's side. They always took me to see her and I would remain at her side for periods of time. She was a tall, bony woman, who knew the Old Testament by heart. She made me repeat it in my childish talk. As I returned home, my mother would ask me: 'What did you do at your grandmother Villanueva's?' And I would answer her: 'We read the words of my father David.'"[70]

7. Death and Eternal Life

Suffering often embitters and brings out harshness or indifference in people, victimized by their own frustration. Gabriela's suffering, like that of Beethoven, had a creative outlet. It was a way of coming closer to God as she passed through the various stages that exist between doubt and belief in eternal life. It was also a way of understanding the suffering of others and comforting them. Her suffering was thus transfigured into universal love.

Throughout her life Gabriela Mistral was obsessed by the idea of death and immortality. Her poems reveal both a fear of death and a yearning for it, a desire to be with God and her dead ones.

She saw in death "a softness" and called it "the lady with deep eyes." She also foresaw in death a way of uniting with Him: "Take me, take me soon. I have not taken roots in the earth of men. You can absorb me with a simple motion of your lips; and with a slight beckoning, you take me in."[71] Twenty years later, in 1938, there appeared the following poem in which she expressed a similar longing:

> *And I give myself fully*
> *to my divine Master*
> *who takes me like*
> *the wind or the river,*
> *and closer than an embrace*
> *He holds me in a clasp,*
> *on a swift flight*
> *we only utter the word Father,*
> *the word my child!*[72]

She experienced divine thirst and realized that her passionate spirit had been shaped by the Old Testament:

> *I was born with a slashed flesh*
> *in the dry heart of Israel,*
> *a Maccabee that brings forth Maccabees,*
> *like the honey of a wasp that turns into mead,*
> *and I have sung as I brought together my hills,*
> *to seize your feet in a clamor.*[73]

But her spirit was also shaped by the New Testament where she found serenity and inner peace. She had come to a spiritual plenitude which made her detach herself from her physical being, in a sublime love for others.

Gabriela had acquired the knowledge of the wise. She stood at the gates of the Kingdom of Peace and saw with the eyes of the soul the promises of the world of the beyond, without ever losing touch with the world of the living.

8. *Two Worlds in One*

Like St. Francis of Assisi, like believers from ancient African tribes, and her own Indians of Latin America, Gabriela could never separate the visible world from the invisible. She did not make a distinction between the natural and supernatural worlds:

"The visible and invisible worlds are one and the same for the wise. For him, the face of the dead brother is within reach, thrown among his toys; for him the elf dwells amongst the leaves of the fig tree; for him, the heaven is interwoven with the earth, like the wolf and the warp of a fabric."[74]

Gabriela insisted on the closeness between this world and the life beyond. She raised the commonplace object and made it a source of beauty. She endowed it with heroic qualities and gave it a soul. She conversed with the salt and called it "Saint"; she compared the saltpeter bed to "the naked Christ of the earth." The earth was to her a reflection of heaven and for that reason she glorified each element of creation. She humanized heaven in order to bring it within the reach of the people, so that they could feel it around them and not know the fear of the unknown. The distance between the two worlds was eliminated as people could touch the intangible. For this reason she admired Jacobus de Voragine, the thirteenth century hagiographer, who in his simplified style of writing was able to bring the saints to the people as friends with whom they could talk:

"Jacobus de Voragine wanted to bring the folklore of the heavens to the earth; he took the blessed from the niches of their churches and placed them in the arms of the people, and he drew the saints so close to his time that the familiarity that exists between saints like St. John the Baptist, St. Anthony of Padua and the Latin people. . . , is due in great part to him. Men and women who are in heaven are somewhat like our blessed grandparents and their glory does not bewilder us because in the 'communion of saints' holiness is a bread which we all share."[75]

She too wrote about the lives of many saints, and her favorite saints were those who did not display their knowledge of spiritual ideas, but who made religion accessible to the people: St. Francis of Assisi (1182-1226) and St. Teresa of Avila (1515-1582), her favorite saints; St. Catherine of Siena (1347-1380); St. Joan of Arc (1412-1431); St. Vincent de Paul (1581-1660); St. Jean-Baptiste Marie Vianney (1786-1859); and St. Theresa of the Child Jesus (1873-1897). She wrote about them because she wanted the people to be enriched by the example of their lives rendered heroic in their every day simplicity. Her fondness for St. Theresa of the Child Jesus, the French Carmelite, sprang from the saint's capacity to come to the people. She was a saint of popular appeal, especially to children:

"Instead of the embellished and bright sky of other saints against which the blessed remain fastened like a blazing symbol, perhaps she conceived of a heaven that would be like a Franciscan tree upon which the righteous are birds that sit on a branch or fly away from it answering the call that beckons them to alight. Or a heaven that would resemble a small teasel rising from the ground, a heaven from which the child saint can detach herself freely and descend upon the beds of the sick with fever, or upon the afflicted who invoke her name."[76]

It is most natural that she should have found in St. Francis a kindred spirit and that she chose him as her special saint. In 1924 she wrote an article about him in which she entrusted him with her love: "But my eyes have rested upon you and want to remain fastened to you, soft ray of the moon, as gentle as a golden thread lost among the morning clouds."[77] Actually, she wrote a poetic biography of her spiritual guide in which she praised his closeness with all created things.

Like St. Francis, she possessed a pure, almost childlike capacity to admire: "For me, one of the things that reveal the quality of the spirit is the capacity to admire, the continuous emotion before beauty, great and small, and before its diverse and sometimes opposite aspects."[78] As a true mystic, St. Francis created names for each element of nature. He knew how to eulogize the things of the earth and how to love them: the water, the furrows, the flowers, the sun, and the fire. God permeated everything in the universe, large or small: "And like few lovers you have the gift for giving a loving name to all that has been created. Francis, the words with which you describe nature are beautiful: you call the fire robust, the water humble and chaste. All of creation loved you; not only because of your sanctity, but because they enjoyed your giving them the names they deserved without excessive effusion or coldness."[79] Gabriela felt his presence in the things of the earth; she shared his way of caring for plants and flowers and animals; she was moved by his manner of holding in his arms a rosebud in order to help it bloom into a beautiful rose: "The flower gazed at him with the golden eye of its gathered stamens and on that day he wrote a song about the joy of the rose when it opens.''[80] She wanted to be endowed with the same gift of love for all things, to be able to pass among them as he did and as does the bee that alights for an instant on a flower and continues onto another.

In an imaginary dialogue between St. Francis and herself, during which she familiarly called him Francis, he explained to her the importance of the senses because through them one can touch, feel, and hear the divine elements of the earth. He told her that her eyes were beautiful because God made them so that she could see the earth; her ears, so that she could hear its sounds. Her senses were like a kite suspended in the air by the thread tied to her hand, coming back to her enriched by its flight. She in turn praised his hair, his eyes, his lips, his smile. She compared him to a fisherman and his smile to a net, heavy with souls. She praised his mother and called her "the Cup of God." He himself fled from acclaim and sought humility: "This is why the road to perfection is so long. If the lily awaited praise each time it shed a petal, it would wait a long time before shedding another. If the singing water awaited to be heard, it would remain motionless on the slope."[81]

Gabriela believed that each of us wears a cord; for her it was a white cord that symbolized St. Francis, the most influential saint in her life:

"Oh Francis, little by little I am tying around my waist a cord like yours. You are the cord that holds me, filling me with joy. It still is not perfect. Help me fasten it with your hands that know all ties. Let your knot be a strong one because I feel that I am still not completely contained in its embrace. I would like its white circle to bind my entire life."[82]

Gabriela simplified her style in order to bring the heavens to the people as Voragine had done. When she imagined an encounter with the Spanish mystic St. Teresa of Avila, she did not embellish her or make her inaccessible to human reach. She described her in a friendly, affectionate way, using diminutives that brought her down to a human scale. This tête-à-tête is very simple and direct: "I look at her and I smile." St. Teresa does not appear with the remoteness one would expect a saint to have, but as the truly lively and warm human being that she was. The very precise portrait that Gabriela makes of her is not at all surprising because for both Gabriela and the saint the spiritual and physical aspects of each human being were significant. Some of the statements on style which she attributes to the saint are an autobiographical disguise. It is Gabriela speaking through her:

"For poetry also comes from love, and not from the thinking mind that struggles with itself: Listen, when you go over and over what you want to say, it rots like a bruised fruit. Daughter of mine, words harden in your mouth and it is because you interrupt the course of divine grace which was coming your way.

"The way to poetry is to cleanse yourself of all will; it is not to thrust ourselves upon God, but to let God thrust creative ideas upon us. Then poetry is born without the blunt edges of things that we make, but with the round smoothness of an orange from Valencia. And let us not forget that it is the doings of the Holy Spirit and that we should not become conceited; nor should it exempt us from hard tasks. To play with children (we who never had any), to play with water that runs without direction, that is poetry.

. . . .

"Mother, you were very fond of water, and you praised it with perfect metaphors.

"—Water, fire, and air are elements that belong to mystics, she said. You have the fire, but not the water. You burn without being refreshed by happiness.

"Beware, fire mixed with earth becomes fuel for passion. To be with God is to be on fire; to descend among people is to reach down for water to experience compassion."[83]

Each time Gabriela read the Gospels, Christianity seemed to her a credo just born; they were written with humility and a youthful force to bring Christ to the people:

"The Gospel is governed by a law similar to that of a nucleus of radium and it is for this reason that in two thousand years it has not lost its strength and it will live on much longer than what some men have mockingly predicted. . . .

"Instead of looking at our religion as something that has come to an end and that has been sealed, let the young people feel it as I do, a religion recently risen in the world, like a new born plant which holds all virtues and the highest of accomplishments."[84]

The Savior was seen as a Child, an adolescent, a young man, but never as an old man. He did not know the wavering concessions of an adult:

"As for the freshness of the evangelists, they wrote their four supernatural documents at a mature age and John, when he was an old man. But the personal contact with the mysterious youth of Jesus had left such a mark on them that their writings do not know the slackness nor the crippling that are part of an old man's style. It is as if they had written the next day after their encounter with Jesus and they still quiver with joy at the surprise and amazement of this first meeting."[85]

Like Seneca years ago, Gabriela believed that style was the language of the soul. She was like a Dutch painter who could bring onto her canvas the common and the sublime to blend them into one. Matter became humanized, the human body had the ethereal beauty of the soul and the soul took on a corporeal or tangible form. Her writing expressed her metaphysical concept of the cosmos. By juxtaposing concrete and abstract imageries she brought a new vision and a new sense of touch which she applied equally to the visible and the invisible, binding the two worlds into one. She visualized the soul as something concrete: "And I do it thinking about the physical and spiritual shape of the soul, for the soul must also have a body."[86] She had magnetic and perceptive powers that enabled her to search and understand people's souls. Like Gabriele d'Annunzio and José Martí she wanted to discover the perfume locked in each soul.

Because the natural and supernatural worlds were one and the same for her, she insisted on the importance of an equal development and care of the human body and soul of children to help bring about a complete, fulfilled human being. For this reason, her journalistic prose is often centered on social reforms and her poetry is an encounter with the powers of the spirit. In her poem "La flor del aire" (The Flower of Air), she tells of her adventure with poetry and calls it the "Woman of the meadow." Gabriela makes of her a queen and lavishes upon her bouquets of yellow, red, and white flowers. She seeks her approval, but the "Woman of the meadow" remains motionless. Gabriela seeks further and discovers the essence of poetry as she goes beyond the visible world of flowers and begins cutting the invisible flowers of the air, now visible to her:

I cut them as if I were
a blind cutter.
I cut from one air and then from another,
making the air my forest . . .[87]

It is a mystic union with poetry, for she follows silently her queen, with her whole being transfigured by the hidden beauties of the spirit.

Her Franciscan concept of the world made her see beyond the visible beauty and gave her a taste of the invisible, of God's boundless beauty. The earth was her dwelling place on her way to eternity:

"Among artists, those who are truly religious have, beside the capacity to create, an intuitive perception of the mystery behind the exterior world. They know that the rose is something more than a rose and the mountain is more than a mountain; they sense the mystic quality of beauty and they find in the softness of grass and of summer clouds the forthcoming touch of the greater softness which lies in the hand of God.

"The yearning for perfection gnaws at their hearts like a wound and just to imagine perfection and to long for it with so much intensity, tells them that the object of their yearning *must exist....*

"An infinite humility invades [the artists] because they feel they are limited receptacles of an unlimited beauty. The unlimited beauty is God."[88]

Like St. Francis, she looked upon nature with a religious fervor. From each particle of matter came forth a vital force, the breath of God. She felt the need to know nature in depth as one knows a friend. She saw in nature a mystery, and she was attracted to what was above and beneath the surface. She listened to the human sounds of the earth. She was not concerned with an ordinary man-made map, but with a map that collected the inner sounds of the earth. She needed full cooperation of the senses—touch, sight, hearing, smell, and additional perception—in order to comprehend nature. She realized upon looking at the sculpture of Michelangelo "The Night" that the earth never sleeps. She gave the earth the characteristics of the great Gaea, the great mother who holds her children in her arms. She believed that the love of mothers for their children parallels the love of the earth for all its creatures, and that the child's communion with the earth is transmitted by his mother.

Gabriela looked at nature both with the eyes of a religious poet, nurtured with images of perfection and beauty, and with those of a woman who had close contact with the land of her birth. The fact that she spent her first years in the Valley of Elqui and that she enjoyed its rural life made her view the earth with the care of a farmer or a gardener who watches the progress of his crops or who is proud of his landscaping. She once wrote: "I like to watch the gardeners as they work. They weed, they embroider, and they breathe over the earth. They are face to face with the earth in a relationship that the laborer does not know, he who beats and turns the soil like the barbarian his wife."[89]

Long before she discovered the importance of St. Francis in her life, she had become aware of the presence of God in the biblical landscapes of her Valley of Elqui. However her personal experience with St. Francis intensified her religious emotion for nature. She would have been angry if someone had called her a pantheist, for she was not one. Within the creation she always saw the Creator:

"Smallness, that of my childhood village, seems to me like that of the Host that thrills and blinds the believer with its round and white shape. We believe that in our region as in the Host there dwells the All; we serve this tiny region beholding in it all the elements of the universe, and that small particle of yearly wheat that will make some people smile or pass indifferently, throws us on our knees."[90]

It was in Monte Grande, as her mother held her by the hand to teach her the marvels of the earth in a fraternal gesture, that she began calling the flowers, the grass, and the little animals by the name of "brother" and "sister." She said of this communion which she had received from her mother:

"Yes, your face was the whole world to me: your cheeks were like the honey-colored hillside and the furrows that sorrow had drawn on each side of your mouth were two small and tender valleys.

"I learned shapes looking at your head, the tremor of blades of grass in your eyelashes, and the stems of plants in your neck which upon bending over me, was a fold of intimacy.

"And when I learned to walk holding your hand, clinging to you like a living pleat of your skirt, I went to the encounter of our Valley."[91]

"In those songs you named the things of the earth for me: the hills, the fruits, the villages, the tiny insects of the fields as if to introduce your daughter to the world and acquaint her with the members of the family. And thus I came to know your gentle and harsh universe. There isn't a single name given to creatures that I did not learn from you.

"Mother, you brought to me the innocent things that I could pick without getting hurt: mint from the garden, a colored pebble, and I would feel through them the friendship of all creatures."[92]

"As I said to you, I carry within me the flesh I borrowed from you. I speak with the lips you gave me and it is with the eyes you gave me that I see foreign lands. Through these same eyes you see the fruits of the Tropics, the sweet smelling and ripe pineapple, and the orange full of light. With my eyes you enjoy the profile of other mountains, sharp like jewels, so different from the red and brazen mountains under which you raised me.

"I thank you on this day and every day for the capacity that you gave me to gather the beauty of the earth as one receives water on one's lips. I also thank you for the plenitude of suffering that I can hold deep in my heart without letting it destroy me."[93]

This love for nature thus sprang from the very layout of Chile as she received the overpowering influence of the Cordillera, the Pacific Ocean, and the profusion of trees, plants, and fruits. After having "possessed" her childhood Valley of Elqui, she was able to see other lands with a perceptive eye and engage in a heart-to-heart conversation with the elements:

"I follow the pathetic appeal of those who, like the Quechua Indian, lie heart-to-heart against the earth in a moment of anguish to forget the turmoil around them and listen to the delicate pulse of the rising sap in the ancestral tamarind tree. These roots are like living anchors deep in the native soil and their vitality is called 'race.' Listening to the silent voice of roots we know how inspiring they are and what they ask of us and this nocturnal dialogue with them is incisive, definite, and with a gentle magic."[94]

It is no wonder then that, as Gabriela came to know the

mountains, the seas, and the trees and flowers from various continents, she would look at them as if they were members of her family, a reflection of God upon the earth. Like the mystics, she enjoyed giving affectionate names to nature and, in so doing, she humanized it or even put an aura around it. The mountain became for her a "Temperamental Creature," "The Sharp One," "An Unyielding Mother under the Sun and the Wind," "Saint of Saints of Our Continent," "A Geological Dragon," "The Granite Beast," "The Tremendous One," "The Centaur of Stone," "The Original Matriarch," "The Sleeping Mother," "The Walking Mother," "The Mother without Knees," "The Venerable Mother," "The Stretched Ark of the Covenant." The sea, which sometimes was masculine or feminine for her, became "The Bossy One," "The Master," "The Great Triton," "The Greatest of Wanderers," "The Most Fickle," "Our Lord," "Our Father," "Father," "Motherly Water," "Marvelous Mother." The tree became "The Champion," "Little Giant," "The Green Cathedral," "The Knight," "The Green Darkness," "Father." Nature took on for her the personality of both father and mother.

On the other hand, heaven held for her the familiar features of the earth. She imagined the Virgin Mary awaiting her at one of the gates to Heaven, cloaked in the blue and white mantle she had seen her with on the altar of her church. She would be her guide in the unknown celestial landscape and would have her mother's face. The Virgin, she said, does not frighten people with her radiance. Her gentle smile and the corners of her mouth make up the gate and its hinges:

"They gave you one of the gates to heaven. For women with tiny hands who cannot reach the door knockers of other gates; for children who go to heaven looking for the face of a woman, with the taste of soft milk in their mouths; for saints, who, between the red and white wings of the Holy Spirit, choose the white. All these enter through the gentle door of daisies.

"Gate of Heaven! I will also seek you in the indecision of the celestial landscape, quivering before its wonder like fog that feels its way with a thousand hands, and suddenly you will appear before me with the face of my mother; the face with which I have always imagined you: green eyes, and on your knees, the long-awaited rest, like a soft seaweed."[95]

"The Queen of Angels," as she called Mary, alleviates the work of miners, the burden of all those who suffer, and gives them confidence and comfort. Her spirit is found in all the beneficent feelings in the world—kindness, patience, tenderness: "To say Queen of Angels is the same as saying the essence of music that produces all notes that float over the universe."[96] In the poem "A la Virgen de la colina" (To the Virgin of the Mount), she expressed this filial love for the Mother of God:

> *It is here beneath the fairness of your feet*
> *that I have come to pass my days.*
> *Your cloak casts a shadow*
> *on my cold and humble door*
>
> . . . .
>
> *If you call me, I shall climb the slope*
> *and will fall upon your rock.*
> *You will hold me to your breast.*
> *Those of the Valley need not know it.*[97]

Her love for her mother often merged with an infinite love for the Mother of God and her feeling for the known and familiar was united with that for the unknown and divine. Gabriela wrote: "I would like to say that I have never lost the lullabies of my first years; I still fall asleep feeling a vague maternal presence and I often recall the words left behind by my mother or by me which led me to the great mysterious embrace of the Divine Mother. From the other shore she gathers me like a broken seaweed that returns to her after being beaten all day long."[98] Perhaps for this reason she seldom found the need to write specifically about the Virgin, for she praised her whenever she wrote of her mother and all mothers. In so doing, she raised motherhood to a sanctified state. The patience of mothers was comparable to that of God, their passion for their children to His for humanity:

"A poor woman rises through motherhood to supernatural life and it is no effort for her, how could it be, to understand the meaning of eternity: man can spare her the lesson on eternity, for she already lives it with intensity."[99]

"Now that I bear a sleeping child, my steps have become silent. And my heart is filled with religion since I carry this mystery within me."[100]

"One never forgets when a man in distress has called us *Mother*. There is great beauty in the lines in which Don Miguel de Unamuno expounds on a new type of motherhood which begins to be known in the world; the kind of motherhood found in the head of a prison or a hospital or the nurses who look after the new born."[101]

In a poetic way, Gabriela compared the mother to an ally of the earth. She herself was its ally. At times she was a daughter who caressed the earth with a filial love seeing in each plant a human gesture, cheek to cheek against the earth; at times she was a mother to the earth and looked upon it as upon a child, for in a maternal love she cared for all of God's creatures; at times she was a sister to the grass or to the trees, or she saw herself as a tree, a shrub, or a humble four-petaled flower. Just as she gave the earth human attributes, she would often borrow the features of plants, flowers, the mountain or the sea to create in her poetry the face of a child. She would thus bring together all of creation.

Gabriela dreamed of seeing houses erected outside of cities so that people would not break away from the aura of the earth:

"Children should be brought up in the country; their imagination is annihilated or becomes morbid if their first nourishment is not the green earth, the limpid horizon, the profile of mountains. Children raised in the country come to the city with the gift of health; their mental faculties are sharp and vivid and they possess the two vital virtues that are inherent to peasants everywhere: strength and serenity that arise from the earth and the sea."[102]

The earth attracted her like a magnet and drove her to believe for a time in reincarnation. Heaven would not be for her a distant place from where she would no longer care for the living. She wanted to remain alive in the games of the children to whom she had dedicated her life, alive in the trees under which they would find shelter. She wanted to walk as a spirit upon the regions she had most loved to rediscover nature through the magic eyes of children and in turn impart to them the invisible beauty which their eyes could not yet see. She would give out spiritual warmth and her spirit would be enveloped with their joyful laughter:

"Many years from now, when I shall be but a tiny, silent mount of dust, play with me, my children, play with the earth my bones

will have become. Should a mason gather me, he will mold me into a brick, and I shall for ever remain fastened to a wall, and I
hate the quietness of a niche. Should they turn me into a brick
for a jail, I shall blush with shame as I listen to the sobbing of a
grownup man; should they turn me into a brick for a school, I
shall also suffer at not being able to sing along with you, at the
start of the day.

"I would rather be the dust with which you play as you walk in
the fields. Press hard upon me: I was once yours, undo me, because I created you; tread upon me, because I did not give you
all the truth and all the beauty. Or just sing and run over me so
that I may kiss your beloved feet." [103]

In her day by day ascent toward God, Gabriela Mistral had
reached the final stage of her life where she did achieve a mystic
union with Him. She laid aside the fires of passion and quenched
her thirst in peaceful waters. She knew that her physical body
stood in the way of the total fulfillment of her soul and symbolically in her poem "El reparto" (Distribution) she gave herself
away, sharing with the needy the body that had once been hers.
Even dead, she would thus remain alive in them, for "from north
to south like a loaf of bread" her message of hope in life would
be their spiritual nourishment. Even dead, she would continue to
be the humble rural schoolteacher who would fight against the
evil powers of materialism:

> *If they place close by me*
> *a born blind girl,*
> *I will tell her, softly, so softly,*
> *with a voice filled with dust:*
> *—Sister, take my eyes.*
>
> . . . .
>
> *Let another take my knees*
> *if hers be fettered*
> *and made stiff*
> *by snow and by frost.*
> *Let another take my arms*
> *if she be maimed.*
> *And others take my senses*
> *with their thirst and their hunger.*

Let me thus be consumed,
shared like a loaf of bread,
hurled from north to south
I shall never again be one.[104]

Stripped of all particles of matter, she had truly become spirit, a spirit like that of the Archangel Gabriel from whom she had borrowed the first half of her name. She could now go to rejoin her Master, uttering as she neared Him the word "Triumph."

I take leave of you now,
I hear the voice of my Master.
He calls me with the sharp thrust
that strikes like lightning:
Sweet and bitter is the call
which bids us to depart.

I came back to save
my little Indian boy
and to tread the Earth
that nursed me upon its breast
and to remember as I walked upon it
the trinity of its elements.
I felt the air, I touched the water
and the Earth. And now I must leave.[105]

Footnotes

INTRODUCTION

1. "Habla Gabriela Mistral en la Unión Panamericana," *Repertorio Americano* (San José, Costa Rica), VIII (August 11, 1924), 322.
2. José Vasconcelos, in Virgilio Figueroa, *La divina Gabriela* (Santiago de Chile: Imprenta "El Esfuerzo," 1933), p. 98.
3. Gabriela Mistral, "Los 'versos sencillos' de José Martí," *Cuadernos de Cultura*, Serie 5 (1939), p. 27.
4. Gabriela Mistral, "Las canciones de cuna," *Repertorio Americano*, V (October 30, 1922), 50.
5. Jorge Mañach, "Gabriela: alma y tierra," *Revista Hispánica Moderna* (Columbia University, New York), III, No. 2 (January, 1937), 110.

CHAPTER 1

1. Virgilio Figueroa, *La divina Gabriela* (Santiago de Chile: Imprenta "El Esfuerzo." 1933), p. 44.
2. Norberto Pinilla, *Biografía de Gabriela Mistral* (Santiago de Chile: Edit. Tegualda, 1946), p. 16.
3. Efraím Szmulewicz, *Gabriela Mistral* (Biografía emotiva) (Santiago de Chile: Editorial Atacama, 1958), pp. 23-24.
4. Oreste Plath, Poetas y poesía de Chile (Santiago de Chile: Talleres Geográficos, 1941), p. 10.
5. Gabriela Mistral, "Las canciones de cuna," *Repertorio Americano* (San José, Costa Rica), V (October 30, 1922), 50.

6. Augusto Iglesias, *Gabriela Mistral y el modernismo en Chile* (Santiago de Chile: Editorial Universitaria, 1949), p. 15.
7. Gabriela Mistral, *Breve descripción de Chile* (*Conferencia en Málaga*) (Santiago de Chile: Prensas de la Universidad de Chile, 1934), p. 12.
8. Gabriela Mistral, *Antología* (Santiago de Chile: Zig-Zag, 1941), p. 18. (Prologue by Ismael Edwards Matte.)
9. José Santos González Vera, "Comienzos de Gabriela Mistral" in *Homenaje a Gabriela Mistral* (Santiago de Chile: Anales de la Universidad de Chile, 1957), p. 22.
10. Mistral, *Antología*, pp. 9-10. (Interview with the mother of the poetess.)
11. Figueroa, *op. cit.*, p. 47. (Letter written by Gabriela Mistral in June, 1933.)
12. Gabriela Mistral, "Valle de Elqui," in Antonio Roco del Campo, *Panorama y color de Chile* (Santiago de Chile: Ercilla, 1939), p. 39.
13. Gonzalo Montes Villapadierna, "Gabriela Mistral nació en el Valle de Elqui." *Ñusta, Revista Femenina Peruana* (Lima, Perú), I, No. 7 (January, 1958), 13.
14. Benjamín Subercaseaux, *Chile o una loca geografía* (Santiago de Chile: Ediciones Ercilla, 1954), p. 93.
15. Gabriela Mistral, "Notas a 'Todas íbamos a ser reinas'" *Tala* (Buenos Aires: Editorial Losada, 1946), p. 156.
16. "Gabriela Mistral recomienda sensibilidad para la diferenciación y la semejanza," *La Prensa* (New York), May 9, 1946.
17. Gabriela Mistral, "El Valle de Elqui", (unpublished).
18. Hernán Pradenas Jara, *Vida y obra de Gabriela Mistral* (Publicaciones del Círculo Literario de Talcahuano, 1954), p. 10.
19. Gabriela Mistral, "Chile", *Lecturas para mujeres* (México: Secretaría de Educación, Departamento Editorial, 1923), p. 172.
20. Mistral, "Chile", in Roco del Campo, *Panorama y color de Chile*, pp. 19-20.
21. Gabriela Mistral, "El mar" (unpublished).
22. Gabriela Mistral, "La Biblia", in Pinilla, *op. cit.*, pp. 65-66.
23. González Vera, *op. cit.*, p. 23.
24. Laura Rodig, "Presencia de Gabriela Mistral," in *Homenaje a Gabriela Mistral.* (Santiago de Chile: Anales de la Universidad de Chile, 1957), p. 289.
25. María de Maeztu, "De la vida de Gabriela Mistral," *El Mercurio,* (Santiago, Chile), February 15, 1925.
26. Figueroa, *op. cit.* p. 155.
27. Pinilla, *op. cit.*, p. 113.
28. Iglesias, op. cit., p. 21.
29. Pinilla, *op. cit.*, p. 27.
30. Rodig, *op. cit.*, p. 284.
31. Iglesias, *op. cit.*, p. 14.
32. Figueroa, *op. cit.*, p. 57.
33. Rodig, *op. cit.*, p. 289; González Vera, *op. cit.*, p. 23.
34. Rvdo. P. Medardo Alduan, "La gran madre", *Ñusta, Revista Femenina Peruana* (Lima, Perú), I, No. 7 (January, 1958), 26.
35. Armando Donoso, *La otra América* (Madrid: Calpe 1925), p. 41.

36. "Sobre Gabriela Mistral," *Alcor* (Asunción, Paraguay), II, No. 7 (1957).
37. Gabriela Mistral, *Las mejores poesías "líricas" de los mejores poetas.* (Barcelona, "Editorial Cervantes," 1923), pp. 5-6.
38. Juan Mujica, "Aventura y gloria de Gabriela Mistral," *Mundo Hispánico* (Madrid, Spain), X, No. 107 (1957), 15.
39. Iglesias, *op. cit.,* pp. 208-210.
40. Carlos Pereyra, "Gabriela Mistral," *España* (Madrid, Spain), August 21, 1920.
41. Gabriela Mistral, "La Estatua de la Libertad", *El Mercurio* (Santiago, Chile), April 5, 1931.
42. Letter from Gabriela Mistral to Rubén Darío, in Antonio Oliver Belmás, *Este otro Rubén Darío* (Barcelona, Editorial Aedos, 1960), pp. 121-122.
43. *Ibid.,* pp. 123-124.
44. *Ibid.,* p. 124.
45. Alone (Hernán Díaz Arrieta), *Gabriela Mistral, Premio Nobel 1945* (Santiago de Chile: Nascimento, 1946), p. 18.
46. *Ibid.*
47. Gabriela Mistral, *Epistolario. Cartas a Eugenio Labarca (1915-1916)* (Santiago de Chile: Ediciones AUCH, Anales de la Universidad de Chile, 1957), p. 55.
48. Gabriela Mistral, "Mis libros", *Desolación* (Santiago de Chile: Editorial del Pacifico, 1954), p. 57.
49. "Les Lettres Françaises ont reçu Gabriela Mistral," *Les Lettres Françaises* (Paris, France), January 18, 1946, p. 2.
50. Arturo Torres Ríoseco, "Gabriela Mistral," *Cosmópolis* (Madrid, Spain), No. 15 (1920), p. 374.
51. Mistral, *Epistolario,* p. 23.
52. *Ibid.,* p. 51.
53. *Ibid.,* p. 22.
54. Gabriela Mistral, a letter to Nataniel Yáñez Silva, in Raúl Silva Castro, *Producción de Gabriela Mistral de 1912 a 1918* (Santiago de Chile: Ediciones AUCH, Anales de la Universidad de Chile, 1957), p. 174.
55. Mistral, *Epistolario,* p. 21.
56. *Ibid.,* p. 25.
57. Gabriela Mistral, a letter to Roberto Mesa Fuentes, in Silva Castro, *op. cit.,* p. 177.
58. Mistral, *Epistolario,* p. 54.
59. *Ibid.,* p. 40.
60. Letter from Gabriela Mistral to Roberto Mesa Fuentes, in Silva Castro, *op. cit.,* p. 174.
61. Mistral, *Epistolario,* p. 43.
62. *Ibid.,* p. 11.
63. *Ibid.,* p. 24.
64. Pradenas Jara, *op. cit.,* p. 12.
65. Mistral, *Epistolario,* p. 36.
66. González Vera, *op. cit.,* pp. 23-24.
67. Mistral, *Epistolario,* p. 39.
68. José R. Castro, "Conversación con Gabriela Mistral," *Crucial* (Mon-

terrey, Mexico), IV, No. 43 (1953).

69. Pereyra, "Gabriela Mistral", *España* (Madrid, Spain), August 21, 1920.
70. Rodig, *op. cit.*, p. 285.
71. Julio Saavedra Molina, "Gabriela Mistral: su vida y su obra," in Gabriela Mistral, *Poesías completas* (Madrid: Aguilar, Biblioteca Premio Nobel, 1958), p. xxiv.
72. Mistral, "Poemas de la madre más triste," *Desolación*, p. 208.
73. Rodig, *op. cit.*, p. 286.
74. Gabriela Mistral, "Máximas", in Pinilla, *op. cit.*, pp. 48-49.
75. Gastón Figueira, "Gabriela Mistral, su significación humana," *Espiral* (Bogotá, Colombia), V. No. 40 (1952).
76. Mistral, *Epistolario*, p. 44.

CHAPTER 2

1. Letter from Palma Guillén to the author, August 31, 1959.
2. Gabriela Mistral wrote some poems for children called "rondas" which were meant to accompany them in their rings-around-a-rosy.
3. Norberto Pinilla, *Biografía de Gabriela Mistral* (Santiago de Chile: Editorial Tegualda, 1946), p. 18.
4. Pedro Prado, Prologue to Gabriela Mistral, *Desolación* (Santiago de Chile: Editorial Nascimento, 1923), pp. 11-12.
5. Rafael Heliodoro Valle, "Aquella tarde con Gabriela Mistral," *Repertorio Americano* (San José, Costa Rica), VI, No. 1 (April 16, 1923).
6. "Gabriela Mistral en España," *Unión Ibero-Americana,* December, 1924, p. 20; Miguel Munizaga Iribarren, "Vida y confesiones de Gabriela Mistral," *Familia* (Santiago, Chile), No. 11 (August 7, 1935).
7. Virgilio Figueroa, *La divina Gabriela* (Santiago de Chile: Imprenta "El Esfuerzo," 1933), p. 101.
8. *Ibid.*, p. 65.
9. María de Maeztu, "De la vida de Gabriela Mistral," *Raza Española,* (Madrid, Spain), (November-December, 1924), p. 54.
10. Gabriela Mistral, "Beber," *Tala* (Buenos Aires: Editorial Losada, 1946), p. 92.
11. Expression used by Gabriela Mistral in a conversation with the author.
12. Laura Rodig, "Presencia de Gabriela Mistral," in *Homenaje a Gabriela Mistral* (Santiago de Chile: Anales de la Universidad de Chile, 1957), p. 287.
13. Gabriela Mistral, *Antología. Edición homenaje a la autora en el año de su muerte* (Santiago de Chile: Zig-Zag, 1957), p. xiv.
14. Gabriela Mistral, *Desolación* (New York: Instituto de las Españas en los Estados Unidos, 1922), p. 243.

15. Figueira, *op. cit.*, p. 36.
16. Gabriela Mistral, *Lecturas para mujeres* (México: Secretaría de Educación, Departamento Editorial, 1923), p. 13.
17. Gabriela Mistral, "Discurso en la Unión Panamericana," *Repertorio Americano,* (San José, Costa Rica), VIII (August 11, 1924), 323.
18. Figueroa, *op. cit.*, p. 161.
19. Letter from Julien Luchaire to Leopoldo Lugones, Buenos Aires, October 23, 1925. Archives of the International Institute of Intellectual Cooperation, UNESCO, Paris.
20. During the meetings held by the Institute, Gabriela Mistral lived in the Hôtel Montpensier, 12, rue de Richelieu, near the Palais Royal.
21. Pinilla, *op. cit.*, p. 21.
22. Letter dated February 3, 1930, from Gabriela Mistral to Benjamín Carrión, in Benjamín Carrión, *Santa Gabriela Mistral. Ensayos* (Quito: Editorial Casa de Cultura Ecuatoriana, 1956), p. 135.
23. Letter dated September 1, 1929, from Gabriela Mistral to Benjamín Carrión, *op. cit.*, p. 131.
24. Letter dated August, 1921, from Gabriela Mistral to Benjamín Carrión, *op. cit.*, p. 124.
25. Collective letter from Gabriela Mistral to the Committee on Ibero-American Classics, August 24, 1933. Archives of the International Institute of Intellectual Cooperation, UNESCO, Paris.
26. *Ibid.*
27. Margot Arce de Vázquez, *Gabriela Mistral, persona y poesía* (San Juan de Puerto Rico: Ediciones Asomante, 1958), p. 13.
28. Figueroa, *op. cit.*, p. 195.
29. Archives of the International Institute of Intellectual Cooperation, UNESCO, Paris.
30. Jorge Carrera Andrade, "La quinta de Gabriela Mistral," *Rostros y climas* (Paris: Edicones de la Maison de l'Amérique Latine, 1948), p. 213.
31. Gabriela Mistral, "Sestri Levante en la Liguria. Italia caminada," *El Mercurio* (Santiago, Chile), May 18, 1930.
32. Letter from Gabriela Mistral to Benjamín Carrión, *op. cit.*, pp. 138-139.
33. Figueroa, *op. cit.*, p. 45.
34. *Ibid.*
35. Letter from Gabriela Mistral to Benjamín Carrión, *op. cit.*, p. 139.
36. Mistral, "Notas a 'Muerte de mi madre'," *Tala,* p. 152.
37. Arce de Vázquez, *op. cit.*, p. 78.
38. Mistral, "La fuga", *Tala,* p. 11.
39. Gabriela Mistral, "Madre mía," *Lagar* (Santiago de Chile: Editorial del Pacífico, 1954), p. 119.
40. Magdalena Petit, *Biografía de Gabriela Mistral* (Santiago de Chile: (Editorial La Salle), 1946), p. 5.
41. Carrera Andrade, *op. cit.*, p. 216.
42. *Ibid.*, p. 217.
43. Letter dated September 1, 1929, from Gabriela Mistral to Benjamín Carrión, *op. cit.*, p. 131.
44. Mistral, "Recados," *Tala,* p. 158.

45. Letter dated October, 1929, from Gabriela Mistral to Benjamín Carrión, *op. cit.,* p. 140.
46. Xesús Nieto Pena, "Conversando con Gabriela Mistral," *Repertorio Americano* (San José, Costa Rica), XXVII, No. 9 (September 2, 1933), 136.
47. Gabriela Mistral, "Oficios de mujeres," *El Mercurio* (Santiago, Chile), December 15, 1929, p. 5.
48. Letter from Gabriela Mistral to Benjamín Carrión, *op. cit.,* p. 138.
49. "La América hispana y la Sociedad de las Naciones," *El Mercurio,* June 8, 1930.
50. Letter from Dominique Braga to Gabriela Mistral, June 16, 1931, addressed to her c/o Palma Guillén, Casella 53, Santa Margherita, Liguria, Genoa. Gabriela was at that time living at 73 Mansion Street in Poughkeepsie, New York. Archives of the International Institute of Intellectual Cooperation, UNESCO, Paris.
51. Gabriela Mistral, "De la Isla de Puerto Rico," *El Mercurio,* January 10, 1932.
52. Letter from Gabriela Mistral to Dominique Braga, January 11, 1932, from Santa Margherita. Archives of the International Institute of Intellectual Cooperation, UNESCO, Paris.
53. Letter from Dominique Braga to Palma Guillén, in Santa Margherita, May 6, 1931. Archives of the International Institute of Intellectual Cooperation, UNESCO, Paris.
54. Letter from Gabriela Mistral to Dominique Braga, November 10, 1932. Archives of the International Institute of Intellectual Cooperation, UNESCO, Paris.
55. Letter sent to Gabriela Mistral, c/o Consulate of Chile, Madrid, July 27, 1933. Archives of the International Institute of Intellectual Cooperation, UNESCO, Paris.
56. June 29, 1933. Archives of the International Institute of Intellectual Cooperation, UNESCO, Paris.
57. Luis S. Granjel, *Retrato de Unamuno* (Madrid: Edicones Guadarrama, 1957), p. 120.
58. Mistral, *Lecturas para mujeres,* p. 11.
59. "Gabriela Mistral, Cónsul de Chile en Madrid," *Revista Hispanoamericana de Ciencias, Letras y Artes* (Madrid, Spain), March 20, 1933, p. 89.
60. Letter from Antonio Oliver Belmás to the author, January 6, 1961.
61. Pedro Juan Labarthe, "La Mistral, Martí y Puerto Rico," *Repertorio Americano* (San José, Costa Rica), XXXI (February 13, 1936).
62. Victoria Kent, "Gabriela Mistral," *Ibérica* (New York), V, No. 2 (Febrary 15, 1957), 9.
63. Victoria Ocampo, "Gabriela Mistral y el Premio Nobel," *Testimonios* (Buenos Aires: Editorial Sudamericana, 1956), p. 178.
64. Kent, *op. cit.,* p. 10.
65. Gabriela Mistral, *La lengua de Martí* (La Habana: Ediciones.de la Secretaría de Educación, 1934), p. 8.
66. Landowners who were given a large number of Indians to work their lands.

67. Gabriela Mistral, "Castilla," *El Mercurio,* July 12, 1925.
68. Kent, *op. cit.,* p. 10.
69. Gabriela Mistral, "Respuesta a un manifiesto de españoles," *El Mercurio,* November 8, 1935.
70. Raúl Morales-Alvarez, "Gabriela come acostada. . . ," *Ercilla* (Santiago, Chile), IV, No. 159 (May 20, 1938).
71. Luis Terán Gómez, "Gabriela Mistral y el ex-presidente Arturo Alessandri," *Alma Latina* (San Juan, Puerto Rico), No. 623 (1947).
72. Iglesias, *op. cit.,* p. 382.
73. Letter from Adelaida Portillo to the author, May 2, 1959.
74. Archives of the International Institute of Intellectual Cooperation, UNESCO, Paris.
75. During her travels at that time, Gabriela Mistral retained her consulate in Lisbon and her address was Avenida Antonio Augusto Aguiar, 191.
76. *Entretiens. Le destin prochain des lettres* (Paris: International Institute of Intellectual Cooperation, 1938), pp. 119-121.
77. *Ibid.,* p. 153
78. Gabriela Mistral en S. Paulo," *A Capital,* XXVIII, No. 26 (1937).
79. E. Rodríguez Fabregat, "Letras de Hispano América. *Tala:* el nuevo libro de Gabriela Mistral," *Esfera,* (Rio de Janeiro), I, No. 4 (1938).
80. "Gabriela Mistral retorna al país," *Ercilla* (Santiago, Chile), III. No. 156 (April 29, 1938).
81. *Ibid.*
82. Joaquín Arizmendi, "Gabriela Mistral, poetisa de América, opina en Argentina sobre Chile, Lugones y Pablo Neruda," *Ercilla* (Santiago, Chile), March 18, 1938.
83. *Ibid.*
84. *Folklore chilien* (Paris: Institut International de Coopération Intellectuelle, Collection ibéro-américaine, 1938), p. 10. (Preface by Gabriela Mistral.)
85. *Ibid.,* p. 13.
86. February 7, 1938. Archives of the International Institute of Intellectual Cooperation, UNESCO, Paris.
87. Mistral, *Tala,* p. 145.
88. Santiago Rivera, "Gabriela vuelve a la patria despues de 10 años. . . ," *Ercilla* (Santiago, Chile), May 13, 1938.
89. Mistral, "Razón de este libro," *Tala,* p. 149.
90. Mistral, "País de la ausencia," *Tala,* p. 90.
91. Concha Meléndez, "América hispana en la poesía de Gabriela Mistral," *Asomante* (San Juan, Puerto Rico), II, No. 2 (1946).
92. Mistral, "Sol del trópico," *Tala,* p. 70.
93. Mistral, "Cordillera," *Tala,* p. 76.
94. Francis de Miomandre, "Gabriela Mistral à Paris," *Les Nouvelles Littéraires* (Paris, France), January 10, 1946.
95. Figueira, *op. cit.,* p. 25.
96. Sidonia Carmen Rosenbaum, "Gabriela Mistral," in *Modern Women Poets of Spanish America* (New York: Hispanic Institute in the United States, 1945), p. 195.
97. Rivera, "Gabriela vuelve a su patria después de 10 años. . . . ," *Ercilla,* May 13, 1938.

98. Gabriela Mistral, " 'Concierto de amor' de Ester de Cáceres," *Revista de América* (Bogotá, Colombia), II, No. 5 (May, 1945).
99. Julio Saavedra Molina, *Gabriela Mistral, su vida y su obra* (Santiago de Chile: Anales de la Universidad de Chile, CIV, Nos. 63-64 (1946), 34.
100. "Puntos de vista. El regreso de Gabriela Mistral," *Atenea* (Concepción, Chile), LII, No. 155 (1938), 177.
101. Raúl Morales-Alvarez, "Gabriela come acostada, a las once está durmiendo. . . ," *Ercilla*, IV, No. 159 (May 20, 1938).
102. *Ibid.*
103. Paul Valéry, *Variété II* (Paris: Editions de la N.R.F., 1937), p. 153.
104. Archives of the International Institute of Intellectual Cooperation, UNESCO, Paris.
105. *Homenaje de la ciudad a Gabriela Mistral* (La Habana: Molina y Cía, 1938), p. 11.
106. *Ibid.*, p. 34.
107. *Ibid.*, p. 35.
108. Susana Redondo de Feldman and Anthony Tudisco, *José Martí. Antología crítica* (New York: Las Americas Publishing Company, 1968), p. 13.
109. Gabriela Mistral, "Los 'Versos sencillos' de José Martí," *Cuardernos de Cultura*, Serie 5 (1939), p. 11. (Given as a lecture on October 30, 1938, at the Institución Hispanocubana de Cultura.)
110. Iglesias, *op. cit.*, p. 381. (Letter from Gabriela Mistral to Gabriel González Videla.)
111. "Carta abierta de Gabriela Mistral a Norberto Pinilla sobre la 'Bibliografía de Gabriela Mistral'," *Repertorio Americano* (San José, Costa Rica), XXXVIII (January 4, 1941), 8.
112. Luis Terán Gómez, "Gabriela Mistral y el ex-presidente Arturo Alessandri," *Alma Latina* (San Juan, Puerto Rico), No. 623 (1947), p. 20.
113. Gabriela Mistral, "Lago Llanquihue," in Antonio Roco del Campo, *Panorama y color de Chile* (Santiago de Chile: Ediciones Ercilla, 1938), pp. 222-223.
114. Paul Valéry, Preface to Gabriela Mistral, *Poèmes choisis* (Paris: Editions Stock, 1946), pp. 12-13.
115. Mistral, "Emigrada judía," *Lagar*, p. 170.
116. Gabriela Mistral, Prologue to Benjamin Subercaseaux, *Chile o una loca geografía* (Santiago de Chile: Ediciones Ercilla, 1954), p. xviii.
117. Gabriela Mistral, "La muerte de Stefan Zweig," *El Mercurio* (Santiago, Chile), March 9, 1942.
118. *Ibid.*
119. Last message from Stefan Zweig, Petropolis, February 22, 1942.
120. *Loc. cit.*
121. Letter from Gabriela Mistral from Rio de Janeiro, November 17, 1943, in Ladrón de Guevara, *op. cit.*, p. 42.
122. This account was related to the author by Palma Guillén.
123. *Loc. cit.*
124. *Ibid.*, p. 43
125. Mistral, "El costado desnudo," *Lagar*, pp. 41-42.
126. Mistral, "Luto," *Lagar*, p. 46.

CHAPTER 3

1. Norberto Pinilla, *Biografía de Gabriela Mistral* (Santiago de Chile: Editorial Tegualda, 1946), p. 78.
2. Matilde Ladrón de Guevara, *Gabriela Mistral "Rebelde magnífica"* (Santiago de Chile: Imprenta "Central de Talleres", 1957), p. 34.
3. Arturo Torres Ríoseco, "Gabriela Mistral, el Premio Nobel y su significado," *Repertorio Americano* (San José, Costa Rica), V (1946), 127.
4. "Jacinto Benavente dice que Gabriela Mistral merece el Premio Nobel," *La Prensa* (New York), November 17, 1945.
5. Victoria Ocampo, "Gabriela Mistral y el Premio Nobel," *Testimonios* (Buenos Aires: Editorial Sudamericana, 1946), p. 178.
6. Pinilla, *op. cit.,* p. 109.
7. María Monvel, *Poetisas de América* (Santiago de Chile: Nascimento, 1929), pp. 13-14.
8. Augusto Iglesias, *Gabriela Mistral y el modernismo en Chile* (Santiago de Chile: Editorial Universitaria, 1949), p. 399.
9. Ted Szulcs, "Gabriela Mistral salió del Brasil rumbo a Suecia" *La Prensa* (New York), November 22, 1945.
10. Augustin Souchy, "El Premio Nobel *"Letras del Ecuador,* II, No. 13 (1946).
11. *Les prix Nobel en 1945* (Stockholm: Imprimerie Royale, 1947) p. 48.
12. *Ibid.* p. 50.
13. *Ibid.,* pp. 61-62.
14. Efraím Szmulewicz, *Gabriela Mistral (Biografía emotiva)* (Santiago de Chile: Editorial Atacama, 1958), p. 116.
15. "Les Lettres Françaises ont reçu Gabriela Mistral," *Les Lettres Françaises,* January 18, 1946, p. 2.
16. Germán Arciniegas, "Gabriela Mistral y Pío XII," in *Temas de Arciniegas, invitación a conversar, leer y escribir,* Osvaldo N. Soto and Cecil D. McVicker, editors (New York: Harcourt, Brace and World, Inc., 1967), p. 63.
17. Juan Uribe Echevarría, "Poesía chilena en el Golfo de Nápoles," *Boletín del Instituto Nacional* (Santiago, Chile), XVII, No. 42 (1952).
18. *Ibid.*
19. Letter from Gabriela Mistral to Matilde Ladrón de Guevara, in Ladrón de Guevara, *op. cit.,* p. 135.
20. Víctor Alba, "La Mistral vista por su amiga y secretaria, *"Homenaje a Gabriela Mistral"* (Santiago de Chile: Anales de la Universidad de Chile, 1957), p. 94.
21. Gastón Figueira, "Gabriela Mistral," *Revista Iberoamericana* (México), XVI (1951), 235.
22. Doris Dana has made an outstanding translation of a selection of Gabriela's poetry. This anthology, *Selected Poems of Gabriela Mistral,* is

a bilingual edition published in 1971 by the Johns Hopkins Press of Baltimore. It is divided into four sections which include selections from four of the books of the Chilean poet: *Desolación*, 1922; *Ternura*, 1924-*Tala*, 1938; and *Lagar*, 1954. This translation was awarded a prize in April 1972 by the American Center of P.E.N. Club. The scroll given to her bears the following inscription: "Doris Dana, in her translation of *Selected Poems of Gabriela Mistral*, the Chilean poet, has made a noble and moving Latin American voice perceptible beyond the Andes. In a work of devotion and skill, which bears the hallmark of fidelity and simplicity, she has avoided imposing her own pattern on a foreign work and has aimed at, and achieved, transparency for the original." Since then, Doris Dana has published books for children based on two fables written by Gabriela Mistral: *Crickets and Frogs* and *The Elephant and his Secret*. These two books, which make her stand out as a most imaginative storyteller, were published by Atheneum in 1972 and 1974.

23. Gabriela Mistral, "Versicle of Peace," *The Americas* (Washington, D.C.), VIII, No. 3 (1951), 281-282.
24. Letter from Palma Guillén to the author, August 31, 1959.
25. Margaret Bates, "Gabriela Mistral's *Poema de Chile*", *The Americas*, XVII, No. 3 (January, 1961), 262.
26. Margot Arce de Vázquez, *Gabriela Mistral, the Poet and her Work* (New York University Press, 1967), p. 49.
27. Ladrón de Guevara, *op. cit.*, p. 164.
28. "Chile y Gabriela Mistral," *Política y Espíritu* (Santiago, Chile), VII (1951).
29. Mistral, "Huerta," *Poema de Chile* (Santiago de Chile: Editorial Pomaire, 1967), p. 52.
30. Mistral, "Copihues," *Poema de Chile*, p. 201.
31. Letter from Gabriela Mistral to Matilde Ladrón de Guevara, *op. cit.*, p. 142.
32. Uribe Echevarría, "Poesía chilena en el Golfo de Nápoles," *Boletín del Instituto Nacional* (Santiago, Chile), XVII, No. 42 (1952).
33. Gastón Figueira, *De la vida y la obra de Gabriela Mistral* (Montevideo: Talleres Gráficos, Gaceta Comercial, 1959), p. 35.
34. "Expresión de admiración y cariño a Gabriela Mistral," *El Mercurio* (Santiago, Chile), September 9, 1954. p. 11.
35. *Ibid.*
36. Poems written for children which were put to music so that children could dance to them.
37. "Expresion de admiración y cariño a Gabriela Mistral", *El Mercurio* September 9, 1954, p. 11.
38. *Ibid.*
39. Gabriela Mistral, "Hay un mundo que camina hacia un futuro mejor" *El Mercurio*, September 9, 1954.
40. "Homenaje de la Universidad de Chile al otorgar a Gabriela Mistral el título de Doctor *Honoris Causa*," *El Diario Ilustrado* (Santiago, Chile), September 11, 1954. (Contains Gabriela Mistral's acceptance speech.)

41. Luz Machado de Arnao, "Yo conocí a Gabriela Mistral" in *Homenaje a Gabriela Mistral* (Santiago de Chile: Anales de la Universidad de Chile, 1957), p. 81.
42. Efraim Szmulewicz, *op. cit.*, p. 121.
43. Doris Dana, "Su causa fue la del niño pobre," *Life en español*, May 1, 1961, p. 48.
44. Uribe Echevarría, *op. cit.*
45. "Desde alta mar Gabriela Mistral saluda a Chile," *La Nación* (Santiago, Chile), September 5, 1954.
46. "Citations of the Recipients in Conferring of Honorary Degrees by Columbia University," *The New York Times*, November 1, 1954, p. 32.
47. Bookjacket of *Lagar* (Santiago de Chile: Editorial del Pacífico, 1954).
48. Mistral, "La otra," *Lagar*, p. 9.
49. Mistral, "El costado desnudo," *Lagar*, p. 44.
50. "Message from Gabriela Mistral on the Occasion of the Anniversary of the Adoption by the United Nations General Assembly of the Universal Declaration of Human Rights," December 10, 1955.
51. Letter from Gabriela Mistral to Matilde Ladrón de Guevara, in Ladrón de Guevara, *op. cit.*, p. 143.
52. Roberto Aldunate, "Tribute to the Memory of Gabriela Mistral, Address Delivered on January 10, 1957, before the General Assembly of the United Nations," *Official Records of the General Assembly, Eleventh Session, Plenary Meetings*, 635th meeting.
53. "Benjamín Cohen lamenta la muerte de Gabriela Mistral," *El Diario* (New York), January 11, 1957, p. 9.
54. "Asamblea NU interrumpe sesión para honrar memoria de Gabriela Mistral," *ibid.*
55. "Sentidas manifestaciones de pesar por la muerte de Gabriela Mistral," *La Prensa* (New York), January 11, 1957, pp. 1,4.
56. *Ibid.*, p. 4.
57. *Ibid.*
58. *Ibid.*
59. "Gabriela Mistral is Dead; Poetess Won Nobel Prize," *New York Herald Tribune*, January 11, 1957.
60. Emilio Mohor, "El último adiós a Gabriela Mistral," *La Nación*, (Santiago, Chile), May 15, 1960.
61. "Santiago despidió a Gabriela Mistral," *El Diario Ilustrado* (Santiago, Chile), March 23, 1960, p. 12.
62. *Ibid.*
63. "Maestros y alumnos rendirán homenaje a Gabriela Mistral," *El Mercurio* (Santiago, Chile), March 21, 1960.
64. "Gabriela Mistral reposa desde ayer en Monte Grande, el pueblo de su infancia," *El Mercurio*, March 24, 1960, p. 19.
65. *Ibid.*
66. *Ibid.*
67. *Ibid.*
68. Salvador de Madariaga, *Homenaje a Gabriela Mistral* (1889-1957)(London: Diamante, 1958), VII, p. 3.
69. Mistral, "Despedida", *Poema de Chile*, p. 244.

CHAPTER 4

1. Gabriela Mistral, "Con Ada Negri," *Repertorio Americano* (San José, Costa Rica), XIII (June 12, 1926), 344.
2. Max Daireaux, *Panorama de la littérature hispanoaméricaine,* (Paris: Kra, 1930), p. 172.
3. Gabriela Mistral, "Una explicación más del caso de Khrisnamurti," *La Nación* (Buenos Aires), August 31, 1930, p. 5.
4. Gabriela Mistral, "Algo sobre el Ecuador," *El Mercurio* (Santiago, Chile), September 22, 1929, p. 5.
5. Maria Monvel, "Gabriela Mistral, franciscana de la Orden Tercera," *Zig-Zag* (Santiago, Chile), May 9, 1925.
6. Gabriela Mistral, "Jacobinismo viejo y cristianismo nuevo," *Nueva Democracia* (New York), X, No. 2 (February, 1929), 4.
7. Gabriela Mistral, "Comentarios a poemas de Rabindranath Tagore," *Desolación* (New York: Instituto de las Españas en los Estados Unidos, 1922), p. 209.
8. Santiago del Campo, "Conversaciones con Gabriela Mistral," *Lo Mejor del Catholic Digest* (St. Paul, Minn.), II, No. 5 (1954), 12.
9. Mistral, "La Cruz de Bistolfi," *Desolación,* p. 6.
10. Gabriela Mistral, in "Lo que dicen maestros y conductores," *Nueva Democracia* (New York), XXX, No. 1 (January, 1950), 22.
11. Gabriela Mistral, in "Lo que dicen maestros y conductores," *Nueva Democracia,* XXXII, No. 1 (January, 1952), 22.
12. Gabriela Mistral, "Silueta de Sor Juana Inés de la Cruz," *Lecturas para mujeres* (México: Secretaría de Educación, Departamento Editorial, 1923), p. 123.
13. Gabriela Mistral, "Infancia de San Francisco de Asís, Capítulo de una vida," *El Mercurio* (Santiago, Chile), October 3, 1926, p. 3.
14. Gabriela Mistral, "Corazones franceses: San Vicente de Paul," *El Mercurio* (Santiago, Chile), November 4, 1928, p. 4.
15. Gabriela Mistral, "Corazones franceses: Teresa de Lisieux, una santa niña," *El Mercurio* (Santiago, Chile), November 3, 1929.
16. Gabriela Mistral, *Poema de Chile* (Santiago de Chile: Editorial Pomaire, 1967), p. 91.
17. Gabriela Mistral, "La Fiesta del árbol. Las colonias rurales. Una plaza de juegos para niños," *El Mercurio* (Santiago, Chile), March 30, 1924, p. 6.
18. "Discurso de Gabriela Mistral al recibir el Premio de las Américas en la Universidad Católica de Washington," *El Mercurio* (Santiago, Chile), December 17, 1950.
19. Mistral, "Canto del justo," *Desolación,* p. 21.
20. Gabriela Mistral, "La buena fe," *El Mercurio* (Santiago, Chile), May 22, 1944, p. 3.

21. Gabriela Mistral, "Cristianismo con sentido social," *Nueva Democracia* (New York), V, No. 6 (June, 1924), 31.
22. Gabriela Mistral, "Giovanni Papini. II," *El Mercurio,* November 2, 1924, p. 9.
23. Gabriela Mistral, "La imagen de Cristo en la escuela," *Repertorio Americano* (San José, Costa Rica), XXXII, No. 540 (May 30, 1931), 310.
24. Autobiographical note, in Gabriela Mistral, *Las mejores poesías "líricas" de los mejores poetas* (Barcelona: Editorial Cervantes (1923), p. 5.
25. Gabriela Mistral, "Unidad cristiana," *Nueva Democracia* (New York), XXV, No. 3 (March, 1944), 8.
26. Gabriela Mistral, "Catolicismo y protestantismo," *Nueva Democracia,* VI, No. 11 (November, 1925), 4.
27. "Gabriela Mistral y la Nueva Democracia," *Nueva Democracia,* VI, No. 1 (January, 1925), 3.
28. Gabriela Mistral, "La imagen de Cristo," *Repertorio Americano* (San José, Costa Rica), XXII, No. 54 (May 30, 1931), 311.
29. Gabriela Mistral, "Recado sobre los judíos," *El Mercurio* (Santiago, Chile), June 16, 1935, p. 2.
30. Gabriela Mistral, "Sobre la xenofobia," *El Mercurio,* December 21, 1948, p. 3.
31. Gabriela Mistral, "Palabras sobre la Paz," *Nueva Democracia* (New York), XXVIII, No. 3 (July, 1948), 31.
32. Gabriela Mistral, in "Lo que dicen maestros y conductores," *Nueva Democracia,* XXVIII, No. 1 (January, 1948), 31.
33. Gabriela Mistral, "Emilia Brontë, la familia del Reverendo Brontë," *La Nación* (Buenos Aires, Argentina), October 5, 1930, p. 10.
34. Gabriela Mistral, "Mis libros," *Desolación* (Buenos Aires: Espasa-Calpe, 1951), p. 40.
35. Gabriela Mistral, "La Biblia," in Norberto Pinilla, *Biografía de Gabriela Mistral* (Santiago de Chile: Editorial Tegualda, 1946), pp. 65-66.
36. *Ibid.,* p. 66.
37. *The Scofield Reference Bible. The Holy Bible,* (New York: Oxford University Press, 1945), p. 44.
38. *Ibid.,* p. 572.
39. *Ibid.,* pp. 707-708
40. *Ibid.,* p. 708.
41. *Ibid.,* p. 1090.
42. *Ibid.,* p. 999.
43. Gabriela Mistral, "Credo," *Desolación* (New York: Instituto de las Españas en los Estados Unidos, 1922), p. 35.
44. Gabriela Mistral, "Proyectos," in M. Guzmán Maturana, *Segundo Libro de Lectura* (Santiago de Chile: Editorial Minerva, 1916-1917), p. 290.
45. Gabriela Mistral, "Motivos de San Francisco. Los labios," *El Mercurio* (Santiago, Chile), March 16, 1924, p. 3.
46. Gabriela Mistral, "Decálogo del jardinero. Cultivemos las flores," in Raúl Silva Castro, *Producción de Gabriela Mistral de 1912 a 1918* (Santiago de Chile: AUCH, Ediciones de los Anales de la Universidad de Chile, 1957), pp. 29-30, first published in *Sucesos* (Santiago, Chile),

April 3, 1913.

47. Letter from Gabriela Mistral to Benjamín Carrión, in Benjamín Carrión, *Santa Gabriela Mistral* (Quito: Casa de Cultura Ecuatoriana, 1956), p. 123.

48. Gabriela Mistral, "Una opinión interesante," in Raúl Silva Castro, *Producción de Gabriela Mistral de 1912 a 1918*, p. 174.

49. Gabriela Mistral, "El pueblo que canta," *Repertorio Americano* (San José, Costa Rica), VI (August 27, 1923), 317.

50. Gabriela Mistral, "Siena," *El Mercurio* (Santiago, Chile), December 7, 1924, p. 9.

51. Gabriela Mistral, "Florencia, II," *El Mercurio*, August 9, 1925, p. 3.

52. Gabriela Mistral, "El 'Moisés' de Miguel Angel," *La Revista Católica* (Santiago, Chile), October 4, 1924.

53. Gabriela Mistral, "Corazones franceses: Juan María Vianney, Cura de Ars," *El Mercurio* (Santiago, Chile), July 14, 1929, p. 5.

54. Gabriela Mistral, "Degeneración del arte cristiano," *El Mercurio*, September 4, 1932, p. 3.

55. Gabriela Mistral, "Artesanos franceses. Bernardo Palissy," *El Mercurio*, October 20, 1929, p. 4.

56. Gabriela Mistral, "El alma en la artesanía," *Repertorio Americano* (San José, Costa Rica), XVI (March 24, 1928), 178.

57. Gabriela Mistral, "En la antesala del oficio," *Nueva Democracia* (New York), VIII, No. 10 (October, 1927), 18.

58. Gabriela Mistral, "El maestro rural," in R. Silva Castro, *Producción de Gabriela Mistral de 1912 a 1918*, p. 153.

59. Gabriela Mistral, "La hora que pasa," *Lecturas para mujeres* (México: Secretaría de Educación, Departamento Editorial, 1923), p. 193.

60. Gabriela Mistral, *Epistolario. Cartas a Eugenio Labarca (1915-1916)* (Santiago de Chile: Ediciones de los Anales de la Universidad de Chile, 1957), p. 24.

61. Gabriela Mistral, "La maestra rural," *Desolación* (New York: Instituto de las Españas en los Estados Unidos, 1922), p. 44.

62. Gabriela Mistral, "Oración del estudiante a la Gracia," *Nueva Democracia* (New York), V, No. 5 (May, 1924), 3.

63. Gabriela Mistral, "Decálogo del artista," *Desolación* (New York: Instituto de las Españas en los Estados Unidos, 1922), p. 207.

64. Letter from Gabriela Mistral to Matilde Ladrón de Guevara, *Gabriela Mistral, rebelde magnífica* (Santiago de Chile: Imprenta "Central de Talleres," 1957), p. 42.

65. Gabriela Mistral, "Corazones franceses: Juan María Vianney, Cura de Ars," *El Mercurio* (Santiago, Chile), July 14, 1929, p. 5.

66. Gabriela Mistral, "Silueta de Sor Juana Inés de la Cruz," *Lecturas para mujeres*, pp. 122-123.

67. Gabriela Mistral, in "Lo que dicen maestros y conductores," *Nueva Democracia* (New York), XXVII, No. 2 (April, 1947), 14.

68. Gabriela Mistral, "Otra carta a un ahijado de guerra, José Rumayor Netto," *Revista de América* (Bogotá, Colombia), II, No. 6 (June, 1945), 350.

69. Gabriela Mistral, "Desde México. El Día de las Madres," *El Mercurio*

(Santiago, Chile), June 24, 1923, p. 9.

70. Santiago del Campo, "Conversaciones con Gabriela Mistral," *Lo Mejor del Catholic Digest* (St. Paul, Minn.), II, No. 5 (1954), 12.

71. Gabriela Mistral, "Comentarios a poemas de Rabindranath Tagore," *Desolación*, p. 211.

72. Gabriela Mistral, "Poeta," *Tala* (Buenos Aires: Editorial Losada, 1946), p. 126.

73. Mistral, "Nocturno de la derrota," *Tala*, p. 18.

74. Words of Gabriela Mistral, in Matilde Ladrón de Guevara, *Gabriela Mistral, rebelde magnífica* (Santiago de Chile: Imprenta Central de Talleres, 1957), p. 169.

75. Gabriela Mistral, "Jacobo de Voragine," *El Mercurio* (Santiago, Chile), April 13, 1930, p. 4.

76. Gabriela Mistral, "Corazones franceses: Teresa de Lisieux, una santa niña," *El Mercurio*, November 3, 1929, p. 4.

77. Gabriela Mistral, "Motivos de San Francisco. Los labios," *El Mercurio*, March 16, 1924, p. 3.

78. Gabriela Mistral, "Escultura chilena: Laura Rodig," *Zig-Zag* (Santiago, Chile), December 18, 1920.

79. Gabriela Mistral, "Capítulo VI. Nombrar las cosas," *Canto a San Francisco* (Santiago de Chile: Imprenta "Dante," 1957), p. 14.

80. Gabriela Mistral, "Motivos de San Francisco. Presencia de las cosas," *El Mercurio* (Santiago, Chile), October 28, 1923, p. 8.

81. Mistral, "Capítulo V. El Elogio," *Canto a San Francisco*, p. 11.

82. Mistral, "Capítulo I. La madre," *Canto a San Francisco*, p. 5.

83. Gabriela Mistral, "Castilla II," *El Mercurio* (Santiago, Chile), July 19, 1925, p. 3.

84. Gabriela Mistral, "Jacobinismo viejo y cristianismo nuevo," *Nueva Democracia* (New York), X, No. 2 (February, 1929), 4.

85. *Ibid.*

86. Gabriela Mistral, "Algo sobre Jorge Mañach," *La Nación* (Santiago, Chile), August 1, 1948.

87. Gabriela Mistral, "La flor del aire," *Tala*, pp. 46-47.

88. Gabriela Mistral, "El sentido religioso de la vida," *Boletín del Instituto de Literatura Chilena*, (Santiago, Chile), III (1963), 21.

89. Gabriela Mistral, "La Liguria caminada: Zoagli," *El Mercurio* (Santiago, Chile), September 17, 1930, p. 4.

90. Gabriela Mistral, *Breve descripción de Chile* (Santiago de Chile: Prensas de la Universidad de Chile, 1934), p. 11.

91. Gabriela Mistral, *"Recuerdo de la madre ausente,"* *Lecturas para mujeres*, p. 27.

92. *Ibid.*

93. Gabriela Mistral, "Desde México. El Día de las Madres," *El Mercurio* (Santiago, Chile), June 24, 1923, p. 9.

94. Gabriela Mistral, *Palabras para la Universidad de Puerto Rico* (Universidad de Puerto Rico, 1948), p. 14.

95. Gabriela Mistral, "Alabanzas de la Virgen," *El Mercurio* (Santiago, Chile), August 23, 1925, p. 3.

96. *Ibid.*

97. Gabriela Mistral, "A la Virgen de la Colina," *Desolación,* pp. 30, 32.
98. Gabriela Mistral, "Colofón con cara de excusa," *Ternura* (Buenos Aires: Espasa-Calpe, 1949), p. 162.
99. Gabriela Mistral, "La madre: obra maestra," *Repertorio Americano* (San José, Costa Rica), XXXVIII (September 20, 1941), 261.
100. Mistral, "Poemas de las madres. La dulzura," *Desolación,* p. 177.
101. Gabriela Mistral, "Recado sobre Victoria Kent," *Sur* (Buenos Aires, Argentina), No. 20 (May, 1936).
102. Gabriela Mistral, "La Fiesta del árbol. Las colonias rurales. Una plaza de juegos para niños," *El Mercurio* (Santiago, Chile), March 30, 1924, p. 6.
103. Gabriela Mistral, "Motivos del barro. IV. A los niños," *Desolación,* p. 190.
104. Gabriela Mistral, "El reparto," *Lagar* (Santiago de Chile: Editorial del Pacífico, 1954), pp. 13-14.
105. Gabriela Mistral, "Despedida," *Poema de Chile* (Santiago de Chile: Editorial Pomaire, 1967), p. 243.